*the*
**TERRIFYING
ART** *of*
**FINDING
CUSTOMERS**

# A Sleep-Deprived Founder's Guide to Revenue

COLLIN STEWART

# the TERRIFYING ART of FINDING CUSTOMERS

PAGE TWO

Copyright © 2025 by Collin Stewart

All rights reserved. No part of this book may be reproduced, stored in a retrieval system or transmitted, in any form or by any means, without the prior written consent of the publisher or a license from The Canadian Copyright Licensing Agency (Access Copyright). For a copyright license, visit accesscopyright.ca or call toll free to 1-800-893-5777.

Predictable Revenue™ is a registered trademark of Predictable Revenue Inc.

MEDDPICC™ is a registered trademark of MEDDIC Academy.

Some names and identifying details have been changed to protect the privacy of individuals.

Cataloguing in publication information is available from Library and Archives Canada.
ISBN 978-1-77458-613-6 (paperback)
ISBN 978-1-77458-614-3 (ebook)

Page Two
pagetwo.com

Page Two™ is a trademark owned by Page Two Strategies Inc., and is used under license by authorized licensees

Cover, interior design, and illustrations by Fiona Lee
Printed and bound in Canada by Friesens
Distributed in Canada by Raincoast Books
Distributed in the US and internationally by Macmillan

25 26 27 28 29    5 4 3 2 1

terrifyingart.com

*For Nikki, Neil, and Joe.*

Introduction 1

1 The Only Thing That Matters 3

2 Finding Product-Market Fit 19

3 Your First Customers 37

4 Getting Ready for Growth 61

5 How to Sell 91

6 Sales Habits 115

7 How to Build Your First Channel 133

8 Four Funnels That Drive Growth 157

9 Hire and Manage Your First Salesperson 181

Tying It All Together 209

Founder Summary 215

Acknowledgments 225

Additional Resources 231

# INTRODUCTION

**Y**ou've built something revolutionary—or at least that's what you believed. Yet when it comes to getting people to actually buy, you're hitting a wall. Prospects smile, nod, and say your product "looks cool," but they never open their wallets.

You might think it's a sales issue—your investors are pushing you to hustle harder and sell more aggressively—but sales remain frustratingly elusive. Trying to understand why people aren't buying feels like staring into a black box. Is it your sales skills? Are you not booking enough meetings? Or worse, could it be that no one genuinely wants what you've created?

Here's the hard truth: It doesn't matter how quickly you build your product if nobody's going to buy it. When it comes to generating revenue, the single most important factor determining your success is identifying a significant unmet need that customers are willing to pay to resolve.

I've been in this frustrating position with my own startups—and survived long enough to help you avoid the mistakes that led to it. Let's break this cycle together and transform polite conversations into paying customers.

## ONE

# THE ONLY THING THAT MATTERS

**Pain is knowledge rushing in to fill a void with great speed.**

JERRY SEINFELD

It was 11 p.m. on a Tuesday night and I was riding my bike home across the bridge again. It was probably raining. Money was so tight that if I got a flat tire, I wouldn't be able to buy a new tube. Rent was due in a few days and I would have just enough cash left over for a giant bag of rice, some vegetables, and a bottle of cheap rum. This was not the glamorous entrepreneurial life I had read about in *TechCrunch*.

It was at this moment that cracks started forming in my "I'm a genius" armor and good advice began to seep in.

A few months earlier I had realized that I was stuck. No matter what we tried, I couldn't get another customer to buy our new software, voltageCRM. It was incredibly frustrating because I had been a strong performer in my previous sales roles and I knew I could close. We even signed our first customer before I had quit my day job. It had almost seemed too easy. But what came easily at first was impossible to replicate. After 18 months of grinding, we still only had one customer. Out of frustration I made a rule for myself that I would be at the office from 8 a.m. to 10 p.m. until I figured out how to find another customer. I had interviewed 150 sales leaders and received mostly positive feedback, and the team had built a number of different minimum viable products (MVPs). But no matter what we did, there was no change in response from prospects. It felt like pushing a wet noodle up a hill.

I had wanted to start a company since I was a kid, and it felt like my dream was crumbling. I remember sketching out video game designs in high school, building business models for *really* dumb ideas in college (such as advertising via urinal stickers), and sketching wireframes for CRMs[1] when I was working as a sales representative. Every time I met an entrepreneur, I would tell them my dream and ask their advice. The most common reply sounded like, "Nothing happens until something has been sold, so learn to sell before you start something."

At the time, the general consensus seemed to be that a great sales team could sell any product[2] regardless of the market conditions. People would point to enterprise products they didn't use or understand as examples: "XYZ software is terrible but they're still growing like crazy—they must have a great sales team." And maybe that was true in the '90s when the internet was still in its infancy and information wasn't easily accessible to buyers. But it wasn't true in 2012 when I started my first company.

Still, I took the advice to heart and spent 10 years selling B2B before I started voltageCRM, my first company. Salesforce was the dominant player in SaaS[3] CRMs, but their interface was a little slow and not super optimized for a sales rep's productivity, especially out of the box. I was frustrated because I understood that SaaS was the right move but didn't love having to wait for Internet Explorer 6 to refresh 17 times every time I created an account, contact, and then opportunity. I was young and wanted to go fast. I thought I could do better.

---

[1] For the non-salespeople: CRMs are customer relationship management programs. You will see this term often, especially since my first big venture, voltageCRM, was one. But it wasn't very good.

[2] For readability's sake I've often used "product" by itself to mean both products and services.

[3] SaaS = Software as a service. You probably know this, but I wanted to be clear I wasn't talking about a Swiss ski resort.

I started working on voltageCRM by sketching out my ideas in a Moleskine. It felt very startup-y. Next, I started hitting up my network for anyone who was open to giving me feedback on what I had come up with. I interviewed around 50 sales and marketing leaders and everyone gave me extremely helpful feedback. One day, a friend of mine asked if I wanted to talk to Bob, the information technology leader at his workplace, where he was a sales rep for Ames Tile & Stone. Bob didn't like Salesforce but also didn't want to string together a series of MySQL databases on his reps' laptops. My sales instincts kicked in when Bob asked how much it was. I remember saying "more than Maximizer but less than Salesforce," which seemed good enough for the first meeting.

I walked out of that meeting excited and terrified. I was excited because it seemed like our first customer was finally within reach but terrified because I still had a full-time job, no technical cofounder, and I couldn't build any of the things I had shown. I called the guy who I had been talking to about being our chief technology officer (CTO). He was super excited and managed to get something going just in the nick of time. We got the deal and I quit my job the day after we cashed our first check from Ames.

Suddenly, I wasn't just talking about starting something. We had a paying customer and I was an entrepreneur. The Ames team loved the product: It was mobile and responsive, and it integrated with their inventory system. It wasn't the perfect vision I had imagined, but it was a start. We spent a few months building out the features that the reps were looking for, and voltageCRM was born.

The high of landing our first customer slowly turned into the grind of trying to sell a CRM to a market that didn't seem to care. We were 50 percent cheaper, but sales leaders didn't think it was worth the risk. We were five times faster to enter data, but salespeople couldn't care less. Over 18 months, we tried to sell every variation you could think of: mobile CRM, niche CRM for different verticals, mobile quoting software, and I even tried to land a deal that would have had us powering a team of 50 cold callers. I had read about customer development but was doing a version where I was half asking questions and half selling something that didn't quite exist yet.

In my roughly 100 "customer development" meetings, I heard a *lot* of comments that sounded like "wow, that's a really smart idea" or "very interesting." I should have realized what they really meant—"very interesting" was my nana's way of politely telling us she didn't like something. If you've read *Never Split the Difference*, you know there is a world of difference between "you're right" and "that's right."[4] What I thought was validation was actually people kindly telling me they'd had enough of me not listening to them.

I didn't have product-market fit. I had a product and a customer, but the market didn't care. I had a valid insight about the future of CRM but was too busy planning my perfect solution. I wanted to solve the sales productivity problem by competing with Salesforce, but prospects were practically begging me to build it to work *with* Salesforce. I pushed on without listening because it didn't align with the way I thought they should solve the problem.

And then, in the summer of 2013, my mentor Roger Patterson said to me, "I just can't wait until you're working on something that has a chance of being successful."

We're both Canadians, and that's about as mean as we're allowed to be, eh. But Roger's words were just the kick in the

---

[4] Chris Voss with Tahl Raz, *Never Split the Difference: Negotiating as if Your Life Depended on It* (Harper Business, 2016).

## Praise for **The Terrifying Art of Finding Customers**

"Too many founders mistake early revenue for product-market fit and scale before they're ready. This book gives founders a disciplined approach to proving demand, testing go-to-market fit, and knowing when to scale. Essential reading."
   **MARK ROBERGE**, cofounder, Stage 2 Capital; founding CRO, HubSpot

"Most founders think sales is about hiring a few SDRs and waiting for results. Collin Stewart rips that myth apart and lays out exactly how to find your first customers, build your revenue team, and avoid the traps that kill most startups."
   **LARS NILSSON**, CEO, SalesSource; ex-VP, Snowflake and Cloudera

"From finding product-market fit to securing early customers and creating a repeatable revenue engine with clarity and precision, this is a reference book you'll pull off the shelf regularly."
   **COLLIN CADMUS**, sales consultant and coach

"Having strong product-market fit magnifies the impact of every sales, marketing, and customer success motion you have. This book nails it."
   **MAX ALTSCHULER**, founder and general partner, GTMfund

"Collin Stewart's approach bridges the critical gap from zero to one, where a founding team's sales skills can blur the signals of product-market fit. These are the essential customer development skills every technical entrepreneur needs."
   **MATTHEW WYMAN**, cofounder and CEO, Okareo

"Packed with real-world strategies and actionable tactics, this guide is your blueprint for turning uncertainty into revenue."
   **JOHN EITEL**, global sales leader

"Collin Stewart's book is your road map to finding quality customers who'll actually fuel your growth, instead of burning cash building products nobody wants."

**MORGAN J. INGRAM**, founder and CEO, AMP Creative

"Collin Stewart provides unfiltered, actionable advice on building a business from the ground up in an engaging and surprisingly entertaining style."

**JOSH SCHWARTZ**, operating principal, Growth Factors

"Collin Stewart's insightful sales book arrives at just the right time. Now I understand how to build a system that makes revenue repeatable, starting with customer development and continuing through building multiple sales processes."

**PAUL D. GURNEY**, cofounder, BigNerve

"For technical founders who've mastered building but struggle with selling, Collin Stewart's book provides the missing link between an excellent product and a viable business. This book delivers the no-nonsense advice of someone who's earned their insights."

**JASON MORRISON**, cofounder, Flowplay AI

"I initially thought this would be a light read, reinforcing things I already knew or had read elsewhere, but it has completely blown me away. So many aha moments."

**SUSAN ABBOTT**, founder, Just Know

"An honest guide to the gritty reality of startup growth. Collin Stewart masterfully blends humor, real-life lessons, and practical strategies to help founders navigate the terrifying journey of finding customers."

**JASON BAY**, CEO and founder, Outbound Squad

"If you're struggling to get your first customers, this book will change the way you think about outreach, feedback, and refining your pitch."

**KRIS RUDEEGRAAP**, CO-CEO, Sendoso

"Collin Stewart lays out actionable steps that make it easy to understand what you can do to successfully find your first customers."

**J. RYAN WILLIAMS**, founder, ANTEATER Media

"Collin Stewart nails it: Before you build a repeatable sales engine, you must bring in those first customers and ensure they love your product enough to stay, pay, and shout about it from the rooftops."

**LLOYED LOBO**, cofounder, Boast.AI and Traction

"Being responsible for growth is terrifying because it never gets easier—just different. Collin Stewart doesn't just capture this chaos—he gives you the tools to survive it."

**COLE FOX**, operating VP, recruiting, GTM, and value creation, Growth Factors

"Collin Stewart has done the extraordinary: Written a book that is one part philosophy, one part practical advice, and several parts wisdom, all combined to produce a must-read for every salesperson and sales leader. Magnificent!"

**ANDREW SYKES**, CEO, Habits at Work

"Collin Stewart masterfully lays out a framework for ensuring your earliest customer development efforts translate into real revenue."

**DREW SECHRIST**, CEO and chairman, Connect the Dots

"This book is like a masterclass in turning panic into profit—read it, and you'll never fear finding customers again."

**LAUREN BECK**, cofounder and COO, Nicest.ai

"Great sales outcomes don't happen in a vacuum; they're the result of strong PMF, skilled reps, and relentless execution. Collin Stewart makes that crystal clear."
**JOEL GRABER**, CEO, Modern Outbound

"Collin Stewart has written the ultimate playbook for founders struggling to turn ideas into revenue. A must-read for anyone trying to crack the code of sales and product-market fit."
**AMIR REITER**, founder and CEO, CloudTask

"Collin Stewart does a fantastic job of showing how his self-proclaimed 'mistakes' and the learnings he gained led to better ideas and proven recommendations."
**JAMIE SCARBOROUGH**, founding partner, Sales Talent Agency

"Finding customers can feel terrifying. But Collin Stewart turns that fear into confidence with a light, engaging, and incredibly practical guide."
**DARIUS LAHOUTIFARD**, founder, MEDDIC Academy

"Scaling sales isn't about hiring more reps and hoping for the best—it's about understanding your market, your buyers, and your numbers. This book walks founders through every step of the process."
**ALICE HEIMAN**, founder and chief sales energizer, Sales Talk for CEOs

"Collin Stewart's wealth of experience and insights learned from helping founders find predictable revenue is as deep and valuable as you'll find."
**SEAN SHEPPARD**, managing partner, FifthRow

"If revenue is the lifeblood of an enterprise, Collin Stewart is the cardiac surgeon of B2B. This book distills a decade under the harsh, fluorescent light of that operating room."
**MARTIN ADEY**, founder, Leadosaurus

ass I needed. I looked up to Roger because he had been there before. He was a successful entrepreneur and had several companies in the works, like Later.com. On the other hand, I was a salesperson pretending to be an entrepreneur in a coworking space surrounded by people actually building things. His comment made me realize that I was so dug into being right that I had lost sight of solving the problem for customers. I was so stuck on validating my idea that I wasn't listening to the real feedback that people were sharing with me. The people I interviewed had a sales productivity problem, especially with their sales development reps, and they wanted something to fix it—as long as it worked with Salesforce.

## The Only Thing That Matters

I had fallen prey to the number one killer of startups: premature scaling. Shortly after Roger's verbal ass-kicking, I came across *Why Startups Fail*, a report by the Startup Genome project.[5] In their study of 3,200 startups, they found that the most common cause of failure was they invested in growth before they had a strong enough product-market fit to get a decent return on investment. Essentially, they were trying to sell something that nobody wanted. Nearly three-quarters of all startups fail due to premature scaling.

It was both embarrassing to realize that my ignorance almost killed the company and a huge relief to know what I needed to do to make it better. It was also nice to know I wasn't alone—but I didn't like being on the wrong side of the statistic.

---

5   Startup Genome, "Startup Genome Report Extra on Premature Scaling," *Why Startups Fail*, August 1, 2011, startupgenome.com/reports/startup-genome-why-startups-fail-premature-scaling.

I understand the urge to scale quickly. As founders, we have a limited time to show growth before the window of opportunity closes. It's like trying to start a fire with a single spark: we need to make sure it catches. The pressure to grow can make us rush and skip steps. An offhand comment from an investor can send a team running—in the right or wrong direction. I have made too many decisions out of a fear of failure instead of slowing down and trying to assess for myself where the crux of the problem really lay. And I have also aided and abetted others in burning cash on premature scaling.

But after Roger's comment, at least I knew what I had to do.

After 18 months and one customer, I made a promise to my cofounders. I wouldn't ask them to write another line of code until we had five paying customers. I had noticed that sales leaders with sales development reps (SDRs) seemed to have the biggest pain and I wanted to validate my hypothesis. I worked out a way to test it manually, but I needed a break, so I booked a surfing trip with my future wife to Costa Rica. I figured that I could take a few months to interview people, run a few tests, and then take some time to recover on a beach while my cofounders, Preston St. Pierre and Francesco Belladonna, built an MVP.

Unfortunately for my future wife and my surfing skills, we didn't make it to Costa Rica.

Even before booking the trip, I had become amazed by what I could see when I finally pulled my head out of my ass and started listening to people. The people I interviewed loved the insight but they hated my solution to their problem. My interviews were with sales leaders and SDRs and they all were struggling with translating their playbooks into something that Salesforce could help them execute in 2013. This was the exact problem we had been trying to solve for the past 18 months—but we had missed a couple of pieces of critical information. Instead of building our own CRM, we needed to work alongside Salesforce. Instead of solving the problem for *every* CRM user, we needed to focus on solving it for SDRs. I had been so close to a breakthrough for so long but I couldn't see it until I started really listening. I was directionally correct but off by just enough to still be wrong.

I worked out how to test the idea with a Wizard of Oz beta[6] by cobbling together a bunch of Google Sheets scripts I copy-pasted from Stack Overflow. Everything was so manual that, when I did the math, I figured I could only handle five customers. My goal was to find five people that would give me $500 to act as an email-only SDR for a month. I wanted to prove that people would pay for this type of automation and that we could generate serious results using the methodology. After five meetings I walked away with *seven* customers—two of the sales leaders were adamant that we had to help their friend's company too, and I couldn't resist saying yes.

When you've been pushing a big rock up a hill for 18 months, getting a response like this is intoxicating.

The manual beta was chaotic but it worked. It worked really well. After we finished, one of our early customers, James Clift, asked for the same but 10 times bigger. James was the guy who recommended I read *Predictable Revenue*, a sales strategy book that would have a huge influence on me, so I didn't want to let him down. I also didn't want to take his money and not deliver, so I managed to talk him down to five times.

---

6   A Wizard of Oz beta is one that gets roughly the same outcome as the future software will with off-the-shelf tools and a bunch of elbow grease. Instead of it all happening the way it *looks* like it's happening from the outside, you're actually in the back end pulling the levers to make it all happen, like the Wizard of Oz. (You also get to shout "pay no attention to the man behind the curtain!" daily, which is the fun part.)

The beta was a turning point for us. Instead of hearing "that's a smart idea," we were hearing "ohhhh, you need to talk to Michelle about this." I managed to pull off 50 interviews in a very short period, mostly powered by unprompted referrals. What this experience taught me was that while sales skills are important, they aren't everything. My sales skills hadn't improved, but suddenly my close rate had shot up. The thing that had changed was our idea. It was the same insight, but we had narrowed our focus to align with what the market wanted.

And the market wanted it. Now we had to deliver it. I couldn't risk losing momentum, so we canceled our Costa Rica trip. I was finally working on something that people cared about, and that was more exciting than a beach.

This experience taught me what should have been obvious: If you're trying to sell something that people don't want, it doesn't matter how good a salesperson you are. And the inverse is also true: When you're trying to solve a problem that everyone cares about, it still doesn't matter how good a salesperson you are. The only thing that matters is finding and solving an unmet need that people place a high value on solving. And when we did this, it spelled the end of voltageCRM... and the beginning of Carb.io.

## OK, There Are Really Three Things That Matter

I lied. There are three things that matter. The first is finding that unmet market need—and the must-have feature to meet the need. The second is finding some people who will give you money for your must-have feature. The third is building a repeatable sales model. Sorry, Shoeless Joe—"If you build it, they will come" isn't true in the real world. You need to find people with unmet needs, learn from them, and then sell to them, and then you need to keep doing all of those things over and over.

It's easy to lose focus when you're consumed with trying to put out fires and finding more people to interview, and everyone in the world is telling you "this is the only thing that matters"—but the "thing" is always different. I don't blame you for trying to scale prematurely, I did it myself. And that's why you're holding a whole book in your hands, not just a notecard. What follows in this book will walk you through the three most important phases of a startup's early journey, paint the picture of what "good" looks like, and poke fun at some of the stupid things I did when I was in your shoes.

Here's what we are going to cover:

### Step 1: Find a Gap in the Market

The first part of the book lays the foundation by helping you identify an unmet need in the market that matches your strengths and vision. I'll cover how to find markets that are likely to have unmet needs, how to measure the size of the opportunity, and what it feels like to have found early product-market fit. By the end of chapter 4, you'll know what to look for and what boxes you need to check to make progress while avoiding premature scaling.

Big ideas:

- the three big shifts in a buyer's world
- finding high-importance, low-satisfaction problems
- using a customer development funnel to find your first customers

### Step 2: Find People Who Will Give You Money

This step's focus is on helping you progress from learning to selling, gracefully and without alienating anyone in the process.

I'll cover my specific process for gradually shifting the conversation from customer development to sales, and I'll share milestones that will help you figure out where you are in the process and what you need to do next. By the end of chapter 7, you'll have your first few customers in hand, a pipeline of warm prospects to work, and a method to measure your readiness to invest in building your revenue engine.

Big ideas:

- quantifying product-market fit
- how to shift from learning to selling
- why founders make the best salespeople, even if you hate sales

### Step 3: Make It Repeatable

The final step closes out the book by taking what you learned about your first customers and using that to build a repeatable revenue engine. I start by walking you through the table stakes you'll need to effectively close new customers, then we'll go over how to find more people to sell to once your network runs dry, and finally we'll close with a look at the basic building blocks of a revenue system. By the end of this book, you'll know how to set up your first customer acquisition channel, create a growth system, and build yourself out of an individual contributor role.

Big ideas:

- what it really takes to build a new growth channel
- how growth is the result of four distinct systems working in unison
- how to build something that sells without you involved

## How to Start

Let's start at the very beginning. Your journey to finding product-market fit begins with the insane decision to quit your regular job and try to create something new. I've done it a few times myself. It took my family a few years (and my company getting to about $1 million in revenue) before they stopped sending me job ads they thought would be helpful. I still remember my old boss Steve sending me redacted pictures of commission checks with the caption, "Yours would be bigger."

So you've made the leap. What now? Before everything, even before you start finding unmet needs, your first step is to find a space to work in. And by that I don't mean an office share. I mean the market space that you're going to focus your efforts in.

When I started my first company in 2012, I chose the sales automation space for two reasons. First, I cared deeply about the end users (salespeople) and thought they deserved better. Second, I believed I had an insight into the industry that I could build around. I'm not sure you need both, but I do believe caring about the end users is essential. This journey you're on is going to suck, sometimes, but other times it'll be great. And sometimes it'll be both in the same day. The thing that kept me going was knowing that thousands of salespeople were struggling because I hadn't built this thing that would help them. It may sound odd, but I cared and I didn't want to let them down. It wasn't a monetary or ego thing; I had been in their shoes and I now had an opportunity to make a small slice of their lives better. That's what kept me pushing forward on those hard days.

Choosing a space isn't something you chisel into stone at the beginning, though. It's part of your initial hypothesis and is likely to evolve as you start interviewing and learning. One of my favorite parts of starting a new company is not knowing exactly where it's going to end up. There's just something fun about the unlimited possibilities in front of you in those early days.

By the way, you don't need a CTO to start a tech company. Many people think you do: If you go to any community for new entrepreneurs it'll be filled with mainly non-technical founders looking for an engineer to build out their idea. I know because I was one of them. I saw a gap, had an idea, and just needed someone to build it. I already had a customer lined up, which put me significantly further ahead than most. But my idea was garbage and we had no business building anything yet. In fact, having a technical cofounder was almost my downfall. My first full-time cofounder, Preston, was able to get something up and running so quickly that we suddenly had something to show. And then, once we had something built—the wrong thing— it slowed us down. We were reluctant to leave the wrong idea behind and jump to finding and making the right one because we had already invested a year in building things.

This doesn't mean you won't ever need a tech cofounder. But a software company isn't started when the first line of code is written, it's started when someone starts working to find a gap. It really picks up momentum when you have something to show customers, and again when that first person pays for it, but you can do an incredible amount of groundwork before either of those things happens. And finding the right set of unmet needs is more important than how you get the product built.

## Creating a Category

You might know Michel Feaster as the cofounder and CEO of Usermind, a customer journey orchestration platform, or from her time at HP when she led the acquisition of Opsware, Marc Andreessen and Ben Horowitz's company. I've had the good fortune to sit down with her a few times, and I credit her with influencing much of my thinking on finding product-market fit—but it is her idea on choosing a space that has stuck with me the most.

Michel explained to me how she created a new market category for Usermind. Michel's Rule of Disruption is that the opportunity to create a category only comes up when there are three or more major changes in a buyer's world. When there is only one change, it's likely to end up as a feature of an existing competitor. This doesn't mean there is no opportunity to create a company based on the change, just that there is likely a limit to the size and long-term competitiveness of the company. So her advice to me was to start by looking for three big shifts in the user's world. When she was starting Usermind in 2013, the three changes she saw were that businesses were buying more SaaS software, all the software had APIs that enabled them to integrate, and new operations teams were being formed to manage them.

Her advice resonated strongly with me because I had spent more than a few years selling to stagnant markets where it was very difficult to pull buyers away from the mainstream competitors. Because there was very little change in the buyer's world, there was no reason to buy from someone who wasn't the big, safe bet they'd worked with before. The risk of going with someone less well known wasn't worth taking because there was little innovation we could offer. The only way we could compete was on price, which is the least fun way to compete. Once you're known as someone who can save people money, it's hard to lose that first impression. At a certain point the only way to reduce the price further is to cut out your commission.

Michel also had pricing in mind, but from a different angle: "I value the ability to set the price point in the user's mind." When you're tackling a problem that hasn't been solved before, there are no pre-existing competitors to anchor the price and terms. You get a chance to start fresh. Her advice was to find a new pain, build a solution around it, and become the market leader in the new category you created.

I sometimes think of a market like a children's ball pit. Instead of uniformly sized balls, there are different shapes and sizes in the pit. The balls represent the market's various customer needs and solutions, and the kids represent change. When there are no kids playing in the pit, everything stays where it is. When one kid runs through the pit, balls will fly around but most of them will stay where they were. When three kids all decide to play in the ball pit, things are going to get crazy. It's this craziness that creates enough change for a new category to spring up.

The best part of starting something new is the ability to go wherever the greatest need is. When you're thinking about which space you want to play in, look for a messy ball pit. Don't be afraid to change pits and follow the chaos. When there is no change in a market, buyers have no motivation to take a risk on something new. But when change is wreaking havoc on the status quo, buyers will do anything to bring some order back into their lives, including taking a chance on a new startup.

# TWO

# FINDING PRODUCT-MARKET FIT

> You can always feel product-market fit when it's happening. The customers are buying the product just as fast as you can make it—or usage is growing just as fast as you can add more servers. You're hiring sales and customer support staff as fast as you can.
>
> MARC ANDREESSEN, "The Only Thing That Matters"

**WE LAUNCHED** Carb.io in the summer of 2014 and grew from $0 to $1 million in annual recurring revenue in a matter of months. It felt like we had just spent two years running through molasses and had suddenly broken free. Things that had previously felt impossible were now easy. New leads were falling out of the sky, sales calls were fun, and everyone in the sales development space seemed to know about us. We were the cool kids on the block for those few months. Our small, bootstrapped startup was competing with companies like Outreach and Salesloft that had raised millions in venture. They were heady times.

If you've never felt strong product-market fit (let's call it PMF), it's hard to read a book and get the same feeling. Historically, the definition of strong PMF was similar to the oft-quoted definition of porn: you'll know it when you see it. While this checks with my experience, I recognize that it's not helpful if you haven't felt it before. The feeling I had when I found it for the first time was like the sensation you would feel after pushing a big rock to the top of a hill for a year and it suddenly started rolling down the other side. Everything just got easier.

The earliest sign of PMF is momentum. When you end your interviews and ask for referrals, people are willing to help. When you're working on something that will help people, you'll find that others will get excited about it and want to share it around.

To me, the moment of finding PMF is a sound. Everyone has a slightly different sound, but on average it sounds like "ahhhh," and sometimes it's followed by "you can do that?" or "oh wow." Often it's a slightly descending note and it almost sounds like relief but not quite. You can sometimes see it too when someone is considering the thing that makes you unique. They'll go silent for a moment or two, pausing to think, and then have this great moment of "I get it." You can see the change in their expression the moment it unlocks for them.

When we were doing our customer development interviews for Carb.io we would ask people, "If we could solve any problem for you, what would it be?" We knew we were onto something special when most sales leaders we interviewed brought up the problem we wanted to solve before we did. It was top of mind because it was the thing they were most upset about not being able to solve. Unlocking this pain point would also lead to a huge increase in productivity on their team. It was so obvious to the people we interviewed, they were mad that something didn't already exist to solve it.

Another sign we were onto something was intros and referrals. The people we interviewed were genuinely excited about what we were working on and would connect us with everyone else they knew who had a similar problem. It didn't always happen in the interviews—sometimes people would just reach out to us cold and say, "I heard from so-and-so that you're working on solving this, can we take a look?"

Our tool wasn't ready for prime time and we told people that, but they wanted to use it anyway. It was so early that half the product wasn't built yet. It was a tool for sending and replying to emails, but you couldn't add or edit your own templates yet—one of our engineers had to create them manually in the back end. We were up front about this, but people still didn't care. It was the magic of PMF.

## What Is Product-Market Fit?

There are many great quotes about what PMF is. One of the most cited resources is Marc Andreessen's essay "The Only Thing That Matters."[7] "In a great market—a market with lots of real potential customers—the market *pulls* product out of the startup," Andreessen says. "The market needs to be fulfilled and the market *will* be fulfilled, by the first viable product that comes along." A great market has such a large buildup of unfulfilled demand that when a product finally appears that can meet it, people flock to it fast.

PMF is the measure of how well your product solves an unmet need in a market. There are three parts: your product, the market, and the fit between the two. The market defines the gap you found and the types of companies and people that experience it most deeply; your product is what you've built to fill that gap; and fit is how effectively your product does this.

In 2021, CB Insights analyzed more than 110 startup failures, and the top two reasons they failed were "ran out of cash" and "no market need."[8] Both of these reflect a lack of PMF. Why? Because the second one is straight-up a lack of PMF, and the first is a knock-on effect of having weak PMF. I'm guessing that the primary reason those companies ran out of cash is that they spent it all on inefficient go-to-market (GTM) investments. This is similar to the Startup Genome project's data from 2011, which I mentioned in chapter 1: 74 percent of the companies they surveyed failed due to premature scaling.

---

7   Marc Andreessen, "The Only Thing That Matters," *Pmarchive*, June 25, 2007, pmarchive.com/guide_to_startups_part4.html
8   CB Insights, "The Top 12 Reasons Startups Fail," August 3, 2021, cbinsights.com/research/report/startup-failure-reasons-top.

The ran-out-of-cash cohort starts to make more sense when you factor in KeyBanc's (originally Pacific Crest) survey on GTM investments.[9] In 2016, the average cost to acquire $1 of new customer revenue was $0.92; by 2021 the number peaked at $1.78. In 2024, the number had cooled off to $1.43. The survey sample was largely venture-capital-backed SaaS companies that had raised a blend of different rounds of capital. I think it's safe to assume these averages represent the success benchmarks, meaning that the 38 percent of companies that ran out of cash in CB's analysis did so because their GTM wasn't as efficient as these benchmarks. When these companies went to raise their next round, their capital inefficiency made them undesirable investments.

People often talk about PMF as if it's something you find and then own, like when kids call "dibs" on a toy or the best seat in front of the TV. This thinking leads founders to believe that once they've "found" it, they have it forever. But PMF isn't something you simply have or don't have. Saying a company doesn't have PMF is like saying a person doesn't have strength—it might be directionally correct but it's not entirely accurate. Instead, PMF is a measure of the strength of connection between your product and the market's unmet needs. It's not a yes-or-no thing; it's about where your product falls along the PMF spectrum from weak to strong.

Finding PMF is like surfing a wave for the first time. At first, you're just trying to stand up without immediately bailing. The feeling you get when you finally stand up is very similar to what it feels like to find PMF for the first time. It's exciting and a little scary. It feels like you're suddenly being carried forward by

---

9   David Skok, "2016 Pacific Crest SaaS Survey—Part 1," For Entrepreneurs, 2016, forentrepreneurs.com/2016-saas-survey-part-1.

something much bigger than yourself. You didn't create the momentum—it was always there, and you just found the right time and place to be to capitalize on it. Eventually, that wave will die down and you'll need to find another to paddle into. That second wave might be the next big market or the second product you launch.

The strength of your PMF is a variable that will ebb and flow over time as your customers and competitors react to your product. It is a measure of how well the product addresses an unmet need in a market at a given point in time. If you change the product or the market, the strength of your PMF will change. If you're changing any of the variables in your PMF equation, it's a good idea to lean on your customer development process to validate your assumptions.

### Product-Market Fit Continuum

**No PMF** (0)    **Weak PMF** (1)    **Strong PMF** (10)    **Uber PMF** (100)

Your job as a founder is to find market gaps. Sometimes that's through interviews, sometimes it's by building something, and sometimes it's by trying to sell the thing we've already built to anyone who'll take a meeting. Once we find a market we can fit into, we need to find a way to profitably reach as much of it as we possibly can.

The pull of a market comes from visionaries and early adopters (I'll discuss this more in chapter 7). These are the easiest folks to sell to because they already understand the problem and have been looking for someone to solve it for them. Finding early success in a market does not mean you'll be able to reach the entire market, however—it means you've found the people who are the most problem-aware. Once you've found all of them, you'll need a profitable and scalable revenue organization to reach the rest of the market. But that's a topic we'll cover later in this book.

## Find Your 10x

There are only two reasons to create a startup: to solve a previously unsolved problem, or to solve an old problem 10 times better than anyone else (I'll refer to this as the 10x principle). There is no middle ground. If you are currently working on a Patreon clone and your differentiator is price, stop what you're doing right now. Not because I don't believe in you or think you can't do it—you probably can. But people won't care. At least, they won't care enough to make the switch.

And that's the most important piece. Just because you *can* build something doesn't mean you *should*. (I really wish I had heard those words 13 years ago.)

People are lazy. I'm so lazy that I'll sometimes check email on my phone while sitting in front of the computer because the phone is a few inches closer. If the computer's bigger monitor can't convince me to move my lazy ass even a little, then convincing a buyer to change how they do something to save 50 percent isn't going to be good enough.

Suppose you want to compete with Patreon. Your options might be:

- Patreon but 10x cheaper
- Patreon but we pay you to subscribe (and the content is maybe 10x better)
- Patreon but we provide 10x more quantifiable value

Or you could just focus on solving a problem that Patreon isn't solving.

Many founders either ignore how lazy people are, are oblivious to how change happens in a company, or overstate how much better their solution is than their current competitors'. If there's one time to be brutally honest with yourself or your cofounder, it's now. Trying to push a product that isn't that different to buyers who have a good enough solution in place already is how most startups end up dying.

When I was trying to sell voltageCRM, salespeople loved what we were trying to do, but we could never get anything implemented because we continuously ran into the objection, "But we just bought Salesforce." Our workflow was two to five times more efficient for the salespeople using it, but we still couldn't make any progress because while our product was great for the users, the managers and economic decision-makers didn't love it. Our product would have been worse for some of the buyers, which is a big reason why we made so little progress. When we focused on productivity for SDRs we found our 10x, and the results speak for themselves.

The way to find unmet needs is simply to ask. Ask a lot of people. But don't just walk up and say, "Hey, what are your unmet needs?" Start with Exploratory Customer Development Interviews.

## *Exploratory Customer Development Interviews*

**GOAL: Find a problem worth solving.**

I use Exploratory Customer Development Interviews when I start exploring opportunities to make sure I'm focusing on the problem that is top of mind for the people I want to target. I use open-ended questions and avoid steering the interview toward my problem space. A great outcome is one where the interviewee brings up your problem space first. An even better outcome is finding a problem space you didn't know existed. If you're surprised, that's a good thing because it means it's not obvious and is less likely to have competitive startups working on the same thing.

It is absolutely critical that you do not share what you're working on before you have asked your questions. When you start by telling someone what you're working on, they will filter their answers to what they think is most relevant to your solution. When you instead start by asking questions, you get to understand what their real, unfiltered pains and struggles are. If you want to feel good and have people tell you you're smart, then tell them your idea first. If you want real feedback, save it to the end.

Each interview has three parts: context, progress, and impact. Use these three as your loose guide to the conversation.[10] You need to strike a balance between asking your questions and letting the interviewee talk. A great customer development interview gets the interviewee talking about their problems and telling stories. Don't be afraid to go off-script or let the person go on a tangent—sometimes these unexpected directions lead us somewhere

---

10  For more on asking good questions and running a good interview, check out *The Mom Test* by Rob Fitzpatrick (CreateSpace, 2013)—and also read the next two chapters of this book, because there are more kinds of interviews coming.

important. But remember: You're looking for patterns in the data, and the data is only as reliable as your interview process. If you use a different set of questions for every person, there will be no consistency. On the flip side, if you only ask your questions, it can put you into checklist mode, which stifles the conversation.

## 1. CONTEXT

To understand the context of the potential customer, I get them to walk me through a day in their life. These questions set the table and direct the conversation to the high-level problem space I want to understand. Here are some questions I learned from Michel Feaster:

- When you start work, what is the first thing you do every morning?
- How many applications do you log into?
- What applications do you love and why?
- Who do you report to?
- What are your annual goals?

These questions work as a setup for the magic wand question: If I could solve any problem for you, what would it be?

The magic wand question helps us understand what pains are top of mind for the interviewee and areas where they would like to make progress. One of the biggest mistakes I made in my earliest customer development interviews was not asking questions that quantified people's pain. Leaving out this crucial detail made it easy for me to continue to pursue something with no future.

## 2. PROGRESS

As I ran more interviews, I got better at asking questions and listening. I could identify unmet needs and articulate them as jobs to be done, but I struggled to get interviewees to clearly articulate their importance. A light bulb came on for me when I read Dan Olsen's book, *The Lean Product Playbook*, and came across the Importance versus Satisfaction Framework. Dan proposed adding two questions to help rank the unmet needs an interviewee mentions.

Afterward when an interviewee mentioned an unmet need, I would ask two follow-on questions:

- On a scale of 1 to 10, how important is this to you?
- On a scale of 1 to 10, how satisfied are you with how you're currently solving it?

These two questions enable you to visualize the unmet needs you've found as a quadrant. What we're looking for are unmet needs that are very important (8 or higher) and have low satisfaction (3 or lower) ratings.

### 3. IMPACT

Once you've found a high-importance, low-satisfaction (HILS) problem, you've found motivation. The next step is to see if that motivation can lead to something meaningful to the company—more revenue, higher profits, or reduced risk. I'll ask questions like:

- If you were able to solve X, how would that impact your department?
- If you were able to solve X, what would that mean to you personally?
- How would that change your role, or your department's?

If you find a HILS problem that can directly benefit your bottom line, you've found yourself something special.

## HISTORY

The history of the problems your customers are facing also matters. Here are some questions that will help you better understand your interviewees and make your life easier when it comes time to build your first customer acquisition channel:[11]

- Tell me about the last time you tried to solve this problem.
- How have others in your organization tried to solve this?
- What resources (time, money, training) went into solving it last time?
- Talk to me about your process for finding a solution.

If they found a solution, ask follow-on questions like, How did you hear about that? (Where did they look, who did they ask, what did they buy, how did they find the last tool they bought, etc.)

This last question will help you understand their buying process and hint at the future demand generation channels you'll need to build. If they haven't tried solving the problem with software, then ask about how they found a related product that they've already purchased.

These questions will help you find unmet needs that might be worth solving. When you think you've found something, it's time to move to Focused Customer Development Calls to validate that assumption. Keep in mind that moving forward in the process doesn't mean you'll never go backwards. Sometimes you'll find a gap that looks real but turns out to be unsolvable or unprofitable to solve. In those cases it's wise to return to exploratory interviews and look for a new gap.

---

11  For more on these questions, see momtestbook.com and also Cindy Alvarez's book, *Lean Customer Development: Build Products Your Customers Will Buy* (cindyalvarez.com/lean-customer-development/), and an interview I did with her over the summer of 2024 (predictablerevenue.com/blog/how-to-run-a-customer-development-interview/). Here's a list of the questions she recommends: lean.terrifyingart.com.

**EXIT CRITERIA**

There are two things I'm looking for before I move to the next step, focused interviews: a clear definition of the unmet needs I've found, and a profile of the people and companies most interested in solving them. I know I'm onto something interesting when most of the people I sit down with list the problem I'm working on as their first answer to the magic wand question. If people are listing your problem but it's not top of mind, that could mean either of two things: Your problem isn't their absolute top priority, or the questions you asked to set up the context are leading them in a different direction.

Remember: The point of running customer development interviews is to find unmet needs, not to get feedback on your idea or prototype. That comes later in the process. For now, we're just looking for problems we can solve.

## How to Find People to Interview

Start with people who will say yes just because they like you. That could be friends, family, or coworkers. My first customer came from an intro from the drummer in my band. He was an outside sales rep for Ames Tile & Stone and put me in touch with Bob, the guy who ran all their technology. He wasn't the VP of sales I was looking for, but the intro did turn into my first sale.

My contacts network in software was nonexistent when I started out, so I joined a coworking space with a bunch of startups, which gave me a decent starting place. I also went to any meetup, industry event, or conference that I thought the people I wanted to interview would attend. When I was trying to get my flywheel going I asked nearly everyone I came in contact with, "Do you know anyone who could give me advice on sales force automation?" (That's what we called sales engagement tools before the term existed. Dang, I'm officially old.)

My first few meetings weren't even close to the right people, but as I progressed, they got better and better. Why? Because at the end of every single interview I asked for another referral. Every layer of referral brought me a little closer to my ideal buyers. If you're talking about solving a big problem that lots of people have, your interviewees are very likely to be open to making intros to others they know who might share the problem. I started with a seed of five people and ended up with 80 by asking everyone for two referrals—if they weren't already trying to force them on me.

But what do you do if you don't know enough people to get your initial flywheel moving? Your options are cold outreach, local events, social media, or ads. You can do a few things to get the snowball rolling, but I recommend starting with cold outreach on LinkedIn. It's the fastest way to get value because it has your contact database, a channel to reach contacts, and a landing page all in one place. Its cost is minimal, compared to the alternatives, and all it takes is elbow grease to get value from it. No fancy automation or complex tooling to set up, and no integrations to fuss with. I like Sales Navigator because of the advanced search functionality.

Here's some messaging I've used recently for LinkedIn:

- **Direct to user:** "Hey Gray—can I pick your brain on sales dev tools? Looking to understand what's good / what sucks about your current tool stack. It's for a future product I'm thinking of building."

- **Direct to user:** "Hey Estefania—can I pick your brain on marketing for the fitness/wellness space? I am just doing research for a product we're considering building and I'd love your thoughts."

- **To founder in the space:** "Hey Sarah—I'm working on a new startup and I could use your input."

You can do this with the free version of LinkedIn, but you will probably need at least a premium subscription to hit the volume you'll need to do it at a decent pace. The process looks like this:

1. Create a search on LinkedIn.
2. Add people from the list.
3. Use the "add a note" feature to drop in your message.
4. Set a goal of messaging 100 people every week until you have your initial seed list.

If your audience isn't active on LinkedIn, I'd recommend following a similar process with low-volume cold email from your personal Gmail. Don't use any sales automation tools because they're overkill and take more work than it's worth to get rolling at this stage. I'm a big fan of simple mail merge tools like Yet Another Mail Merge for Gmail—I used them when starting Carb.io and Predictable Revenue and go back to them every time I need to send a low volume of highly targeted emails. You'll likely be fine as long as you keep your volume low (below 100 a week) and your messages limited to asking for help or advice. Don't try to pitch or sell in these emails—that will dramatically increase the risk of deliverability problems.

Pro tip: Take it from someone who's sent millions of cold emails, if your target person isn't responding to your outreach, try reaching out to people adjacent to them and asking for help finding the right person. This works for two reasons: First, people are much more likely to help when it's not going to cost them time; and second, sometimes you were targeting the wrong person and opening up the aperture can lead to surprising results.

Local events, meetups, and conferences are going to be the easiest for getting yeses because it's much easier to get a referral from someone you met in person. On the other hand, it's harder to get the courage to go to events like these. I've spent my life in sales and I still don't love bouncing from group to group asking for referrals. I'll do it, I just don't love it. Additionally, events with your target buyers might not be physically or financially accessible.

Social media can be great if you know the platform well and there are active communities that discuss your problem space. Finding a Facebook group or subreddit focused on the same problem can be like striking gold. The key here is to build up a reputation as a part of the community before you start asking for feedback. This way, when you engage you don't look like someone just trying to copy-paste links to their own threads. You'll know what an average post looks like, why people hang out there, and how people usually engage. The best social media advice I've received is to create content unique to the platform. Copy-pasting the same blog post to LinkedIn, Reddit, and Instagram is a great way to show those communities that you're not an active member.

### One More Trick: Just Ask

One of the best ways to figure out how to find more interviewees is simply to ask. Next time you're talking to someone, don't just ask for a referral—ask for their advice on getting in touch with more people like them. The last time I went through this process, someone pointed me to two industry conferences as well as the main professional organization for their field. They suggested I reach out to both the organization's leadership (at the national level and in each state chapter) and the speakers who were presenting or had presented at those conferences.

This approach opened doors I'd never even have known existed. Industry leaders and conference speakers tend to be well connected, and because they're often passionate about their field, they're surprisingly willing to introduce you to other people who share the same pain points. By asking "Where else should I look?" rather than just "Who else do you know?" you transform each interview into a mini–research engine for finding your next batch of prospects.

# THREE

# YOUR FIRST CUSTOMERS

> In theory, there is no difference between theory and practice; but in practice, there is.
>
> REMARK OVERHEARD AT
> A COMPUTER SCIENCE CONFERENCE[12]

**O**UR FIRST 10 PAYING users for Carb.io came from customer development interviews. We didn't plan it this way. The people we interviewed wanted the product so badly they didn't give us a choice.

If nobody you interview wants to buy what you have, go back to exploratory interviews—you haven't found their most important problem. If you'll allow me a silly metaphor, imagine you're developing the world's first fire extinguisher and you interview 50 people who are currently on fire. You'd expect them to want your product as soon as possible... right?

Which is also why you should expect to get your first customers from these interviews, and why you should go back to the people you've interviewed to ask them if they want to buy what you've built. If you've interviewed people who are on fire, and you've developed a fire extinguisher (let's just imagine that these people are somehow still alive), wouldn't it be kind of you to go back to them and see if they want to try your solution? It seems rude to just leave them burning.

And yet, many founders I talk to don't go back to the people from their customer development interviews to ask if they want

---

12  From *Pascal: An Introduction to the Art and Science of Programming* by Walter J. Savitch (Benjamin/Cummings Publishing Company, 1984), 366.

to buy. Why? Because they believe "that's sales' job." It really isn't. It's not just that you already have a relationship with the people you interviewed. Until you've closed $1 million in revenue, there is still valuable information that you're learning from every interaction with a potential customer. There is nothing more important at this stage than getting as much customer feedback as you possibly can. How do you know which features to build without feedback from actual customers and prospects? It's rare that you get it 100 percent right on the first try. And when you add a salesperson in between you and the end customer, you insulate yourself from their feedback. You're still getting it, if you ask, but it's being processed by someone else who doesn't understand the problem space as well as you do. It's like buying audiophile headphones and then putting a piece of wood between them and your ears. There's nothing wrong with salespeople—eventually you'll need them—but every layer of people between you and the source reduces the fidelity of the information. In the early stages of finding your first customers, you, like Aerosmith, don't want to miss a thing.

Many founders feel like they can—or even should—offload or outsource sales as soon as possible. They are wrong. Achieving your first $1 million isn't a sales function, it is the product of your customer development process. A good sales conversation is nearly identical to that process—you just ask for money at the end. Moving on from interviewing to selling is the culmination of everything you've learned and your first opportunity to test your product idea in the wild. Remember, a true customer relationship is created with a financial transaction; if we skip the sales work, can we truly say we've engaged in customer development?

Don't think that "sales professionals" will automatically sell better than you can. You are the expert on the problem space. There is nobody else in your company who can understand and empathize with customers better than you.

So when should you offload sales to someone else? Let me put it this way: Imagine a race where you don't know where you're going. What's more important, speed or information about where the finish line is? This blind race is your journey to solidify your product-market fit. Hanging on to the sales role will give you more information about the finish line, while offloading it will improve your speed. When is the right time to trade off information for speed? That's a question only you can answer, but when you're still in the customer development phase, well within your first $1 million, my answer is, "Not yet." Don't worry, we'll get there... in the last chapter of this book. For now, stick with the program.

## Welcome to the Whitewater

So now you're in customer development, but somehow you're also already in sales. It feels like you're trying to assemble your whitewater raft while you're already in the rapids. It's scary here, and many founders either get stuck hanging back or try to get ahead too quickly and get soaked instead.

This is the Whitewater Passage. Your product isn't good enough to justify a large investment yet, but it's developed enough that you expect to have some momentum by now. There's something here that's sellable but it's not achieving its full potential value yet. You're caught between the need to keep learning and the need to start selling. The challenge is that it's hard to do both effectively at the same time. If you focus too much on learning, you may never find your first customers; but if you focus too much on selling too early, you risk alienating the people who have been helping you identify unmet needs.

The key to making it through the Whitewater Passage is momentum. At the end of every call, I always have an ask, and one of my go-to strategies is asking if they know anyone else

I can interview. This simple question is my secret to securing more and higher-quality customer development interviews. I also typically ask if they'd be open to another call. The details of this second ask vary depending on where I am in the process, but it's always intentional and designed to keep the conversation moving forward.

Many founders and venture capitalists I've talked to will say this is the stage where you need to just sell more. They believe this wholeheartedly because it's what made them successful. But they're falling for survivorship bias—most startups that try this end up sinking because they're investing in growth with weak PMF. When you switch into sales mode too early, you lock yourself into a fixed path when you should still be exploring, which is the mistake I made with voltageCRM. If customers buy, that's a bonus, but the one thing you need more than revenue at this point is insight. With only a few customers, you don't know enough about the market yet and your product isn't fully developed. Their feedback is crucial for improving it.

Additionally, taking a sales posture too early can mislead potential customers. If you project too much confidence in your product, it may be disappointing for them when they realize how early-stage your company actually is. This can damage the trust you've built with the prospect. You also risk giving them the impression that your first version is the final version.

But on the other hand, if you don't start generating revenue, you won't have a company left to support the development of your product. If you get stuck in "it must be perfect" mode, spending all your time building the perfect first version, you'll run out of cash before you can take it to market. So you can and should sell as a part of your customer development process. But it needs to be handled differently than in a pure sales process.

How do you do that? The primary goal of a customer development call is always learning, but you can have a few calls to action at the end. In addition to always asking for a referral to someone else to talk to, I ask if they want to see what we've built or, if we're super early, they want me to get in touch when we have something ready to show. The ratio of learning (asking questions) to talking about your product should be 98 percent learning to 2 percent your product. Going too hard on the sales process at the end of customer development calls can make people feel like they've been pulled into a bait and switch, which is not a great place to start with a prospect. Asking for advice can't be—or even appear to be—a sneaky way of starting a sales conversation. Someone is giving you some of their time to be helpful, and you need to respect that.

## The Customer Development Funnel

I use four distinct types of customer development interviews to systematically guide the process from learning about prospects' problems to introducing a solution. These are: Exploratory Customer Development, Focused Customer Development, Paper Feedback, and MVP Demo. Each type builds on the last, gradually shifting the conversation from understanding the customer's pain to validating your solution and ultimately selling it. If you can walk a prospect through each of these stages, you're positioning yourself well to convert them into a customer.

Here's how the process works:

1 **Exploratory Customer Development**: This is where it all begins. When I'm just starting, every conversation is exploratory. As discussed in chapter 2, the goal is to uncover potential pain points, understand the broader problem space, and identify opportunities worth pursuing.

2 **Focused Customer Development**: Once I identify a promising gap in the market, I transition to focused interviews. These are designed to validate that the pain I've found isn't unique

to my initial sample but is shared by a larger audience. Focused interviews give me confidence that the problem is worth solving.

3. **Paper Feedback:** After confirming that the problem is widespread, I test my solution concept with lightweight mockups of the core value-creating features (they don't have to be on real paper). This stage helps me validate that my proposed approach will be 10x better than existing alternatives. It's where I refine my solution before investing in development.

4. **MVP Demo:** Only after confirming the potential for a 10x improvement do I move to build a minimum viable product. The MVP Demo stage is all about gathering feedback on what's been built and understanding what's missing to fully address the customer's needs. Often, I'll go through several rounds of these demos, iterating until there are no glaring gaps. Once the feedback stabilizes and the solution is solid, I invite the prospect into a sales conversation.

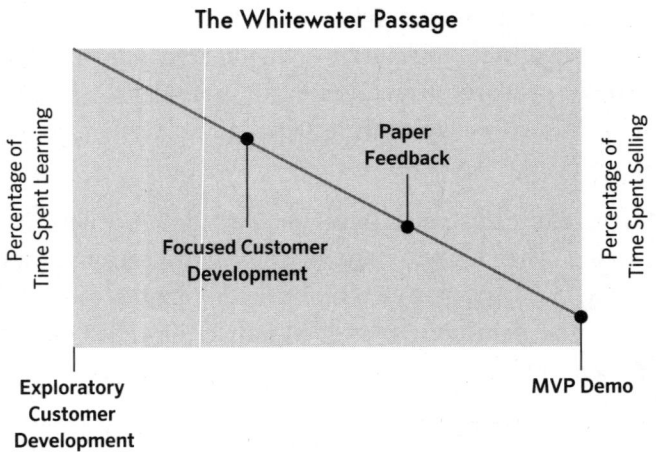

The Whitewater Passage

This structured approach not only ensures that I'm building the right thing but also keeps the momentum going as I steadily progress from learning to selling. By consistently having an ask at the end of every call and following this laddered interview process, you'll maximize your chances of turning prospects into paying customers.

A note on why I use so many interview types: The goal is to help my prospect and me slowly walk from a learning relationship to a revenue relationship. Using multiple interview types helps me keep a clear separation of learning and selling in my process. However, if a prospect is trying to pull your solution out of you and wants to use or buy your product right away, then feel free to skip ahead. The only word of caution I'll leave you with is this: It's almost never a good idea to give an early prospect a demo before you've done a focused interview with them. I'll leave it up to you to strike a balance between listening to the prospect and standing up for your process. When I was doing customer development for Carb.io, I could see people getting excited; they would interrupt my questioning and ask to see what we had. It can be hard to resist their excitement, which is definitely a good signal, but if you're there to learn, make sure you do that first and then do show-and-tell. It's hard to put the toothpaste back in the tube once you've revealed what you're working on.

## *Focused Customer Development Calls*

**GOAL: Verify that the gap you found is their number one problem.**

Use Focused Customer Development Calls to complete your understanding of the problem space.

These interviews will follow a similar process to the exploratory interviews, with the key difference that you start the conversation by steering the interviewee toward the gap. When I did this for Carb.io, it sounded something like "Today I'd like to talk about how you handle sales force automation for your sales development team" or "If I could solve any problem for you related to your sales development team's productivity, what would it be?" Questions like these focus the attention of the interviewee on the specific problem space you found in your exploratory interviews.

In these interviews, you're trying to understand the impact filling the gap would have on their organization and all the variables that would go into your solution. You might have multiple Focused Customer Development Calls with a company or individual that is showing a great deal of pain and an interest in you solving it. To explore the full problem space, it's a good idea to interview other buying influences (economic, technical, user, manager) in addition to your internal champion.[13]

Now is also the time to figure out how your target audience finds and buys products like the one you're thinking of building. I'll ask questions like:

---

13  For more on buying influences, see Robert B. Miller and Stephen E. Heiman, with Tad Tuleja, *The New Strategic Selling: The Unique Sales System Proven Successful by the World's Best Companies* (Grand Central Publishing, 2005).

- How did you hear about that tool?
- What did your buying process look like?
- What was the total cost to the organization to get that implemented (software, implementation, internal labor)?

**REVENUE**

This is where I'll try to gauge what their price sensitivity feels like. My goal is to bucket their interest into a few price categories so I can figure out what my sales model will need to look like to reach them. The buckets I typically use are $1k, $10k, $50k, and $100k because they give me a rough idea which channels will be profitable. This also helps me flush out opportunities where the users have a huge amount of pain but their organization is very unwilling to solve it. I ask questions like this: "If I were to ask for $1,000 a month to solve this, would you throw me out of the room?" There are a variety of ways you can ask these questions. If you're looking for a deep dive on pricing, check out this blog post by Steven Forth: pricing.terrifyingart.com.

**FEATURES**

Once you've understood the context of the problem space, it's time to figure out the big chunks that you'll need to build to solve it. If they've brought up feature ideas already, I'll list them out and ask the prospect to pick the top three. If they haven't, I'll ask them to give me the top three things a solution would need to handle for them to consider the problem solved. This will give you a sense of what you'll need to build *and* give you a reason to get back in touch with them when you build those features.

**CALL TO ACTION**

The call to action at the end of each meeting is a *very soft* ask if they'd like to take a quick look at what you've built so far. Make sure you only take a minute to show them what you have. The goal is to get them excited enough to commit to the next meeting, not to start collecting feedback on the spot. If they seem interested in adopting, I'll book another time and make it clear that the next meeting will be more of a feedback session. It sounds something like, "I'll show you what we're thinking of building and you can tell me what you like and what's missing." This sets their expectations to be ready for a prototype demo and hints at an eventual transition from learning to selling.

**EXIT CRITERIA**

Moving on from Focused Customer Development Calls generally means we're going to start building a solution, so the bar is high.

We've validated the unmet needs. Eighty percent of interviewees who fit the ideal customer profile have the pain, consider it high importance / low satisfaction, and the math makes sense for solving it.

We've validated the business model. The core math that I'm always paying attention to is whether I can charge users enough for the product to justify the investment it will take to make them successful.

Here's my rough math:

> X = Total value created for the user × 5–10% = My value capture target
>
> Y = What type of team will be required to find, acquire, and make customers successful? And what will that team cost? = My cost to acquire a successful customer
>
> Z = How big is the total market? How long will I have to exploit my temporary advantage? Will I be able to parlay this into adjacent markets or use cases? Is there an opportunity to build power? = My total opportunity size

X and Y tell me if I'll be able to profitably acquire successful customers. Note that I include the cost of onboarding and customer success teams here along with anything else that will be required to help the customer get the ultimate value from my product.

Z helps me understand if this is something that's bootstrappable or venture-backable. I know I won't be able to fully make the case one way or another yet, but I like to start thinking about it at this stage. It helps me align with the founders on whether or not to pursue the opportunity. Sometimes you want to knock it out of the park, but other times you're happy just getting on base.

## How to Know if You Don't Have Strong PMF

A few years ago, a friend of mine was working as the chief operating officer at a startup and introduced their revenue leader to me. They had a huge need for what we did and we had unique experience in their particular vertical, but when it came to sign the deal they ghosted us. Three months later, my friend introduced me to their new sales leader and we restarted the process. This was their fourth sales leader within a year. The company wasn't growing, so the founders kept firing their sales leader.

If a company isn't growing, it's not always the fault of the revenue leader. It's more likely poor PMF. Unfortunately, when a company is struggling, the revenue leader often gets fired. This sets the company back, costs a good amount of cash, and doesn't make progress on the goal. It also sucks for the sales leader who unjustifiably lost their job. So, for your good and the good of your sales team, learn to recognize weak PMF.

"You can always feel when product-market fit isn't happening," Marc Andreessen wrote. "The customers aren't quite getting value out of the product, word of mouth isn't spreading, usage isn't growing that fast, press reviews are kind of 'blah,' the sales cycle takes too long, and lots of deals never close."[14] Even if you have a product and some customers, you can still have weak PMF. Your ability to efficiently find more customers is driven by how much pain there is in the market and how well you address it. The greater the pain, the greater the opportunity. If you're having trouble adding go-to-market channels profitably, the problem might not be the channel—it might be your product.

I didn't hear a lot of "ahhhh"s when I did my interviews for voltageCRM. I got a lot of encouraging words, smiles, and people telling me they thought my idea was really smart. I wrongly assumed that if people thought it was a dumb idea they would tell me. Most people are too kind in these situations. They want to be helpful but they don't want to give you money—and encouragement is free. If you're not hearing "ahhhh"s, watch out for the silent no's: people saying they like your idea, or some other niceties that don't make them lean in and ask more questions. Or just remember my nana: "very interesting" means "this is shit."

But I love building a path to the first 100 customers. I've done it multiple times for myself and in helping other founders, and it is one of the most rewarding experiences. I dislike trying to help people understand that they don't have strong enough PMF to warrant investing in go-to-market. Founders are rarely excited to hear it, especially when they thought they could give me some cash and their growth problem would go away. But if you have a growth problem, only the founder can solve it. The good news is that you can solve it as long as you follow the process and put the work in.

---

14  Marc Andreessen, "The Only Thing That Matters," *Pmarchive*, June 25, 2007, pmarchive.com/guide_to_startups_part4.html.

The number one question I get from new founders is, "How do I find my first 10 customers?" The first question I have for them is, "How many people from your customer development process have signed up?" If they've interviewed 100 perfect prospects and zero were interested in paying, that's a pretty solid signal that their PMF is weak—and their "customer development" interviews weren't developing real customers. Your first 10 customers should come from your customer development process. And your next 10 should come from referrals from the first 10. If you're not getting that, throwing money at it won't help. There's nothing there for the money to help.

In the years leading up to writing this book I made thousands of sales calls trying to convince founders not to invest in growth because they weren't ready. These conversations never went well even though I was trying to tell them *not* to give my company money. They were especially hard because we were both right. And wrong.

The founders were right because they had a product, a market, and some customers. If customers are paying for it, using it, and getting value out of it, it's hard to argue that there isn't some form of product-market fit. So, to channel my inner Jeff Foxworthy, you might not have strong PMF if:

- You cannot clearly articulate your three hypotheses: market, need, and solution.

- Nobody from your customer development interviews wants to buy.

- Your interviewees aren't willing to give you referrals.

- Your current customers aren't open to making referrals.

- Your current customers are from a variety of different verticals.

If these resonate, you might benefit from strengthening your PMF. The things you can do to start that are:

- Go back to Exploratory Customer Development Interviews to find a deeper pain connected to the problem you want to solve.
- Look at your data: Are there subsegments of people who get more value from your product than others?
- Go ask your customers and interviewees for advice—make sure you listen to them—and then ask for a referral. If they're hesitant, ask why. That's usually where the real feedback lies.

That last bullet isn't a sneaky way of getting referrals; it leverages the social pressure of asking for a referral to get real feedback. If it generates referrals for you, great, but the reason to do this is to solicit feedback.

And, yes, it means go back to people you've talked to before. Here's a conversation I've had more than a hundred times in my role as CEO of Predictable Revenue:

> *Founder:* We want to hire you to help us find customers!
>
> *Me:* That's great! How many do you have now?
>
> *Founder:* None, that's why we are talking to you.
>
> *Me:* Interesting, tell me about your customer development process.
>
> *Founder:* We talked to hundreds of companies and they all loved it.
>
> *Me:* Great, why didn't any of them buy?
>
> *Founder:* We didn't ask them / The product wasn't ready yet / They weren't ready.

> *Me:* Why don't you go ask them now?
>
> *Founder:* It was a few months ago / We did and they weren't interested. (Or just an uncomfortable silence.)

There are a few reasons why people don't go back to their early interviewees. One is that their idea has evolved since their early conversations and it might not be relevant to the interviewees anymore. I can see this possibly being true, but I'd still go back to the early people to explain the change and get their feedback. Another reason is that they didn't really find anything in the interviews. This was my experience with voltageCRM — I didn't go back to the people I interviewed because I knew they didn't want it. I was building my solution for somebody else, and unfortunately, that somebody else was fictional in my case. But I suspect the third reason is the most common one for not going back: They don't know they should or they don't know how. If you're stuck, go back to the customer development funnel and invite folks to the next stage of interviews.

## Finding First Tracks

While I was writing this chapter, I sat down with a subscriber to my Founder's Edition newsletter[15] because I was looking for examples of early journeys that were less straight-line than Carb.io's, and he was in one of the hardest yet most fun parts of his startup journey. I'll call him Greg because he asked to remain anonymous. He had found his first 30 customers and was trying to decide if he should stay focused on improving the product or

---

15  Visit newsletter.terrifyingart.com to see all my posts and subscribe if that's your thing.

switch his focus to revenue. Greg runs an educational technology platform, they're 18 months into the journey, they've raised $1 million, and they've kept the team small.

While I was thinking about our conversation, I listened to the episode of the *Invest Like the Best* podcast that featured Boyd Varty talking about the art of wildlife tracking. As I listened, I couldn't help but think of Greg's situation. He was pursuing something interesting, hadn't found the path forward for his business yet, and needed to find the signs that there might be a track there. Boyd talked about finding the first tracks that you need to string together to create the overall trail. When you're first learning to track, you don't know what these early trails look like because you don't know the characteristics of the terrain. Eventually, you train yourself to see the path forward, developing what he calls track awareness. Something clicked for me. Greg didn't need advice on how to follow the path; he needed something to help him find his first tracks.

Finding product-market fit isn't a straightforward path. Everyone's route to it will look different, but the first tracks, the signals that there's something exciting just up ahead, will be similar. Here are three sets of first tracks I've used in the past:

**Product Usage:**

- Great = Net-negative churn—any revenue contraction is more than covered by the expansion of current accounts
- Good = Everyone who's paying for it is still using it
- Bad = Greater than 20% annual churn

**Referrals:**

- Great = 10% of active customers have sent at least one referral

- Good = Any number of referrals to customers that close
- Could be bad = No referrals[16]

**Customer Sentiment—the "how would you feel if this product didn't exist anymore" question:**

- Great = Very disappointed
- Good = Somewhat disappointed
- Bad = Not disappointed (it isn't really that useful)
- Real bad = I no longer use it

Not all "great"s are created equally. The Customer Sentiment "great" is the best gauge but it's also the easiest to trick yourself with. In my experience, when customers say they are happy but aren't buying more or sending referrals, it's a sign they are *not* happy and don't want to share their feedback. In those situations, I hadn't earned their trust because I'd demonstrated that all I cared about was our vision and not their pain. I needed to build trust by showing vulnerability and demonstrating that I was receptive to feedback before I could get them to open up with their real feedback.

Feedback quality is a fourth gauge you can use, but it's even more subjective than customer sentiment. When I'm building something new, I like to have weekly check-ins with all of my customers, moving to monthly when we have more than 10. I have three priorities in these meetings: ensure everyone is able to use the product, build our relationship by providing any coaching they might need, and get feedback on what parts of

---

16 *Could* be bad because some industries and customer segments just aren't keen on referrals.

our product need to be improved. The first two goals ensure that the customer is able to use and get value out of the product, and the last one tells me how they're really feeling about it. (It's actually the timescale of the feedback that tells me the most—when they start asking for features like integrations, which they know will take longer to build, I know they're thinking ahead about how to embed our tool in their systems and processes.)

**Feedback Quality**

- Great = Feedback and product ideas that could help them build this into their workflow
- Good = Feedback on bugs that are driving them crazy right now
- Bad = No feedback or ideas for things that are not aligned with your vision

Feedback on bugs sounds bad, but it's a sign that they care enough about your solution that they are mad because it doesn't work better. You definitely have work to do, but your users care and that's the most important thing. No feedback or misaligned feedback is an indication that your users either don't care or don't want to solve the problem in the same way you do. It might be bad or it could be a miscommunication; either way, it's valuable to understand why. Feedback on things you could do in the future, or what customers would need to integrate your product more deeply into their process, are the best kinds of feedback. They show that your customer has accepted your product into their life and are thinking long-term about your relationship.

When you're collecting feedback, don't forget about your customer development question framework—most importantly, "How important is this to you?" and "How satisfied are you with how you're currently solving it?" The combination of the two will help you sort and prioritize the information. It's also good to follow up on their feedback with additional questions to help you understand the impact your solution will have on them. Sometimes the feedback will be for small quality-of-life improvements, but other times it can open up entire new markets for you.

So, what should Greg do?

Let's get the obvious scenarios out of the way first. If everything is "great," he should focus on revenue. If everything is "bad," he should focus on improving the product. The minimum bar to switch focus from product to revenue reminds me of *Breaking Bad*'s character Saul Goodman, whose name is a riff on "it's all good, man." If your results are all at least "good," man, it could be time to focus on revenue. But while Greg could switch his focus at that point, if he instead focuses on product until he has at least one "great" under his belt, it will make everything easier when his company switches to revenue. So, if you're sitting on the Saul Goodman line, ask yourself: Do you want to shift to revenue now, even though it may be harder to find customers? Or can you afford to be patient and invest in finding something "great"?

Feedback is only helpful if you are open-minded enough to hear it. Something I struggled to do was listen and keep my emotions out of it. I remember being so pissed off at Jason Bailey (a serial entrepreneur and dude trying to be helpful) at a startup event that I reached up to the stage and grabbed the mic from him to counter the reasons why he thought voltageCRM was a bad idea. Jason is an entrepreneur with multiple successful exits. He was also a cofounder of the accelerator I was trying to get into. I had gone to the event looking for feedback from people just like Jason, but I wasn't happy with what he had to say. I understand now that he was just trying to help me, but his feedback felt like an attack on everything I was working on. If he was right, I was just wasting my time trying to build something that nobody would want. And he was right. I was breathing smelly air. And I should have kept a better grip on my emotions.

## Are You Ready?

When you are trying to find product-market fit, there are three big milestones before you graduate to the go-to-market phase:

1  Building something that solves the problem
2  Getting your first few customers
3  Confirming that your product solves the problem 10x better (and is a must-have)

The first thing I try to figure out is if there are enough unmet needs to justify an MVP. If my customer development interviews go well and are producing referrals to people who share the pain, I'll invest the time to build an MVP. The most important piece at this stage is unmet needs. You don't need to solve them perfectly, but there needs to be a large set of them. Referrals are the best indicator of how easy it will be to sell your product—if referrals are plenty, it's a good sign.

To justify investing in the full version of the product, I need to be confident that I can optimize it for the right combination of the three hypotheses: market, need, and solution. Making drastic changes to any of these after you've invested in building a first version is much more expensive. I like to see my referrals from people who are actually using and enjoying the product. The best indicator for me is when referrals remain strong after people have used it for a while. Referrals at this stage demonstrate that our users are confident in our ability to solve the problem, even if it isn't all the way there yet.

The last thing I try to confirm before moving into full sales mode is revenue. It doesn't have to be full pricing, but if the product is at the 50 percent point on our road map, we should be able to command roughly 50 percent of the full price. It's OK to give your early customers great deals as long as you are very clear how long those deals will last. The revenue from early customers won't be significant in the long run, but their referrals and references will be.

One of the ways I've screwed up this transition is by not being super clear about when they're going to have to pay—and when they're going to have to pay more. It really sucks to lose one of your favorite customers because of poor expectation-setting in the early days. When we first launched Carb.io, we offered unlimited access to the platform plus a huge number of email credits for $500 a month. What we didn't think about was that there were real costs to adding more users, especially before our infrastructure was battle-hardened. It made sense for us to charge $500 for one to 10 SDRs, but one of our customers wanted to add all of their 100-plus salespeople to our platform. We could have handled it, but it would have taken the resources of the entire company, which wasn't worth doing for only $500. The problem was that some idiot (me) put "unlimited users" in their proposal and our point of contact wanted to hold us to it. One careless word and a lack of an end date on the contract term created a situation where a happy customer ended up going in a different direction. Were they being unreasonable? A little bit. Was it entirely my fault? Yup.

# FOUR

## GETTING READY FOR GROWTH

**If at first you don't succeed,**

**then skydiving definitely isn't for you.**

STEVEN WRIGHT

**W**HEN CARB.IO started taking off, it *really* took off. Every customer we onboarded gave us two or three referrals, a good percentage of them would close, and then the cycle repeated itself. We were selling a tool for outbound sales teams even though we didn't have such a team ourselves because we couldn't even keep up with our own inbound demand. We also had three well-funded competitors looking over our shoulder (Apollo.io, Outreach, and Salesloft), and they were quickly passing us in functionality and go-to-market (GTM) capabilities. The pressure felt enormous, so I did what I knew best: put my head down and just kept pushing. That decision is likely my biggest blunder. We had found strong product-market fit and we had clearly built something that people needed. However, we were missing some key pieces... and it was all about to come crumbling down.

Our servers were on fire because we had insisted on taking on as many customers as we possibly could, as quickly as we could. I wanted to see that unicorn growth curve. And we did—but only for a few months. I used to joke that we had hockey-stick growth, but after that initial growth spurt, the stick flipped—which made it a plateau. We were bootstrapped, and trying to keep up with well-funded startups wasn't something we'd be able to do. But I pushed us on anyway. I had stopped asking users for feedback about where the product was and instead was trying to hang on to customers by shipping the same features as my competitors.

Looking back, I had three possible paths in front of me: keep pushing for parity with funded competitors as a bootstrapped company; raise some money for fixing our issues and continue competing in the same market; or stay bootstrapped and cut the scope to a niche level, where we could have prospered.

I tried the first option and it didn't work out well. In short, if you never pay off your technical debt, eventually it'll bite you in the ass. I kept pushing the team for one more feature so that we were at feature parity. What I didn't realize was that if we didn't focus on fixing some of the stability problems, it was going to start costing us customers. When you are paying for a tool to help you send emails and it takes a week for that batch of emails to be sent, users won't be happy—and churn will follow.

Our first sign that things weren't great was that referrals started to slow. We were still so bogged down in customer conversations that it took us a few weeks to even notice. One week my calendar was fully booked, the next it was only 80 percent, then 50 percent, and then suddenly we had to scrape and hustle for every reply from a prospect.

What had changed was the public opinion of our tool. While people loved the user experience, they just couldn't trust a system that took that long to send emails. The resulting word of mouth surrounding our product turned from overwhelmingly positive to negative in a matter of weeks, and eventually we were forgotten about. This huge wave of demand had started rolling away from us and we were never able to recapture it. Fortunately, our bacon was saved by the services business we had built to fund the development of Carb.io. Those services slowly evolved into what Predictable Revenue is today, a company focused on helping founders build their first revenue team.

## Being Responsible for Growth Is Terrifying

Being responsible for growth is terrifying. It's OK to admit it. I'm 13 years in and I still get that pressure feeling between my chest and my stomach when our pipeline feels a little bit thin. I remember thinking everything would magically change when we hit $1 million in annual recurring revenue and I would finally be happy. It didn't, and I wasn't. As soon as we hit $1m, I set my sights on $2m. Every time we hit a major milestone I would be happy for that day, then wake up the next day and add another million to my expectations.

Every company starts at zero. Trying to grow from zero to $1 million is nearly impossible. Then once you've pulled off this impossible feat, you need to find a way to replicate your success and make it profitable. For me, trying to go from $0 to $1m felt like learning how to water-ski without skis on and the boat's already doing 30 knots. All I could do was hang on to the rope and hope I'd eventually figure something out. But getting from $1m to $5m was like trying to figure out how to water-ski to Mars. I had a rough idea of what I needed to accomplish, but I had no idea where to start.

There's nothing that can really prepare you for the breadth of the founder role. A successful founder journey from zero to your first million requires the equivalent of becoming a semi-pro athlete in three different sports: sales, product, and revenue. I started with a background in sales and had to learn product and how to build a revenue organization. No matter what your background is, there are going to be things you'll need to learn—and some people may have to learn all three. It sounds daunting, but it's doable.

Growth doesn't just happen. It can't be bought or outsourced. You have to get your hands dirty and figure it out for yourself. Growth is an outcome, the thing that happens when every team in the company is firing on all cylinders. It can feel fickle: One moment you're pushing a big rock up a hill and the next it's rolling back down so fast you can't keep up. You'll have many of these moments, sometimes in the same day.

It's easy to get caught up in the excitement of finally seeing growth and forget to ask why. And when the growth suddenly slows and you don't know why, it can be terrifying. You can lose a lot of sleep trying to figure out where to apply your attention when nothing is working. You've spent months or years pushing this big rock up a series of hills and now you're braced against the bottom of it, trying not to let it roll backwards and crush everything you've built. I've been there.

Whether you have raised venture capital, are bootstrapping, or are somewhere in between, getting the timing of your GTM investments right is critical. Too soon and your investments are wasted; too late and you'll miss targets and run out of cash. If you're venture-backed, you have numbers that both current and future investors want to see within a very short window. If you're bootstrapped you likely have limited cash flow, and every dollar poorly invested is a dollar not in your pocket. We all have limited resources and short windows of opportunity.

And I'm going to ring the product-market fit bell again: The strength of your PMF has a direct impact on the effectiveness of your GTM efforts. In the earlier days of Predictable Revenue, 80 percent of our non-software revenue was outsourced SDR work, and a couple of times every year we would land a new customer that, no matter what we did, would get results that were 2x our benchmarks. Every time I'd investigate, there would be nothing special about their messaging, targeting, or tactics. They just seemed to have a product that the market *really needed*. Their market was filled with huge numbers of customers with unmet needs. Customers were pulling the product out of them, even if it was still a janky beta filled with bugs.

## The Growth Formula

The stronger your PMF is, the higher your return will be on every $1 invested in growth. I hate to bring math into the equation, but here we go anyway. Here is the Growth Formula:

> Growth = Cash invested × PMF strength × Revenue execution

### Cash

Cash represents time and effort. You only have a fixed amount to invest to get to the next milestone. This applies if you are venture-backed, bootstrapped, or somewhere in the middle. It doesn't matter how strong your PMF is if you run out of cash. You might swim as fast as Michael Phelps, but if you run out of air, you won't reach the finish line.

### PMF Strength

The strength of your PMF is not binary. It exists on a scale from weak (launching another vanilla CRM system in 2012) to strong (Uber launching Uber Eats in 2015). The strength of your PMF will determine the return you get on your revenue investments. The greater the unmet need for your product, the easier it will be to beat a path to customers.

Imagine you're a musician and your job is to write a hit song. When people love your song it's easier to get the word out and the song will get more plays. The effort you put into producing a great song is like the effort needed to strengthen your product-market fit. Everything else serves as an amplifier that enhances your song's sound, but it doesn't add a hook that gets the audience to sing along.

### Revenue Execution

The strength of your revenue execution can be measured by your theoretical maximum monthly recurring revenue (MRR), which is:

> MRR Ceiling = New customers added each month × Average monthly revenue per customer × Average customer lifetime

I like to look at these numbers as weekly snapshots to see if I'm trending up or down. The only way to grow your company is to pull on one or more of these three levers.

Most people's first reaction to growth challenges is to pull on the first lever. They think, "If only I could talk to more prospects, I could double my revenue." This might be true, but there are a few steps that come before it. If one of the numbers falls off, it can have a dramatic impact on the others. To achieve growth, you need all three working together.

Our revenue formula for Carb.io looked something like this:

> 10 new customers a month × $2k average MRR/customer × 4-month lifetime = $80k MRR

We shot up to $83,333 MRR very quickly and then got stuck. In the early days, every client would refer a friend. But when the platform started struggling to send emails, those referrals stopped because people were recommending Outreach or Salesloft instead. We very quickly dropped from adding 20 customers a month to 10 and then 5, and stayed there for quite a while. This is what premature scaling looks like. Churn had caught up to us and we had to get back to pushing.

## Power

For companies beyond the initial startup phase, power, as defined by Hamilton Helmer in his book *7 Powers*, comes into play.[17] According to Helmer, power is your ability to generate persistent differential returns in a market—in other words, earn steady profits. Each power comes online at different phases in a company's growth, so make sure you're poking your head up and thinking a few years down the line every once in a while. They are as follows:

**Scale Economies:** The more you produce, the cheaper each unit becomes—making it tough for smaller rivals to catch up.

**Network Economies:** Each new user increases the product's value, creating a winner-takes-all effect that later competitors can't easily challenge.

**Counter-Positioning:** Adopting a new model that the established company can't imitate because it would hurt their current business.

**Switching Costs:** Making it hard or expensive for existing customers to leave, forcing competitors to offer big incentives to pull them away.

**Branding:** Leverages emotional appeal and reassurance so that customers are happy paying more than for an unbranded alternative.

**Cornered Resource:** Gaining special access to a crucial asset—like top talent (the elite 0.001%) or patents—that competitors can't easily match.

---

17  Hamilton Helmer, *7 Powers: The Foundations of Business Strategy* (Hamilton Helmer, 2016).

**Process Power:** Creating a deeply embedded, hard-to-replicate way of working that leads to better products or lower costs over time.

Here's the equation:

> Growth = Cash invested × PMF strength × Revenue execution × Power

Looking back to the CB Insights survey, 54 percent of startups found some form of product-market fit, beat a path to market, and then got crushed by a competitor. Three of the main reasons they failed were: they got outcompeted (20 percent); a flawed business model (19 percent); and pricing (15 percent). But the root reason is likely power. They failed because their competitors had power that enabled them to generate higher profits and reinvest those profits in their business more efficiently.

Strong product-market fit produces a temporary advantage by exploiting a market opportunity that your competitors haven't seen or been able to execute on. But your success will show them the path and highlight the value in the market. There will be followers. Power is what will protect your profit margins and enable you to outearn your competitors.

## Keep Learning

Two big decisions I made cost Carb.io its future: not raising a round of venture capital (to keep chasing our well-funded competitors) and not narrowing our product scope to a niche. When I think back on it, finding a niche we could have dominated would likely have given us the best chance. So the question is, what could have helped me get there?

As my buddy Kareem Mayan likes to remind me, "You nailed the hard part (finding PMF) and screwed up the easy part (building a product)." Our product was too broad for our development capacity. We bit off more than we could chew and needed to find a smaller bite. What kept making me want to push for broad features was that multi-channel sales development was the new hotness, and Outreach and Salesloft had just launched calling features. While most of our users wanted to go multi-channel, I suspect that not all of them cared about the phone. If I would have sat down for more feedback sessions, I suspect I could have found a path forward by focusing on users that only cared about email.

Here are the feedback sessions that I should have made good use of—and that *you* should make good use of.

## *Paper Feedback*

**GOAL: Confirm your proposed solution is 10x better than what exists today.**

Once you've established that the unmet needs you've identified are the top problem shared by people in your target group, begin exploring potential solutions. At this stage, I use paper prototypes to validate that the way I'm thinking of solving the problem will resonate with users and effectively address their needs. You don't need to use real paper, just whatever is going to be fast for you and help communicate your idea. Please don't write code yet. Writing code tends to create momentum and excitement, which can be dangerous if it's in the wrong direction. In my experience, it's much easier to click delete on an ugly prototype in Balsamiq than to throw away a bunch of prototype code.

This phase is about testing concepts before any development begins. I'll create mockups or sketches that represent the key elements of the solution and use these to conduct feedback sessions. The aim is to ensure that if we build it, the solution will indeed solve the problem—and that users will be eager to adopt it. Feedback from these sessions gives me the confidence to move forward, knowing the team's time and effort will be well invested.

In these discussions, don't present the entire solution. Focus only on the top two or three features or aspects that align with the unmet needs identified during earlier conversations. It's critical to keep the feedback loop open and listen more than you talk. These early discussions also help me refine my understanding of what 10x improvement looks like from the customer's perspective.

**EXIT CRITERION**

Stop using Paper Feedback when users have validated that using the solution, as designed, will be 10x better than what they're doing today.

## *MVP Demo*

**GOAL: Validate that the prototype you've built solves users' problems and achieves the desired 10x improvement.**

Once the Paper Feedback phase confirms you're on the right track, it's time to build and test your minimum viable product. The MVP Demo phase involves presenting your first working prototype to users, gathering feedback, and iterating based on their input. This step closes the loop, ensuring that what you've built not only meets their expectations but delivers a transformative improvement.

During the MVP Demo, focus on the features that matter most to the user. Before the call, review your notes from previous sessions to identify their top three priorities or requested features. Use this information to tailor your demo, presenting only those specific features and keeping each presentation brief—no more than one to two minutes per feature. After each mini-presentation, pause to collect feedback.

Avoid the temptation to show everything you've built. Prospects care about whether your product solves their problem, not the details of an admin panel or extra features they didn't request. Keep the demo simple and targeted.

If the demo goes well and the prospect is engaged, this is the moment to transition into the sales process. Early on, I typically let the first few users try the product for free to gather real-world feedback. Once even a few users are consistently finding value, I start asking for money.

**EXIT CRITERION**

When users confirm that the solution achieves the 10x improvement you aimed for, you're ready to move on from the MVP Demo to broader product development and a gentle push into revenue.

## Finding the Fat Dads

One thing I have learned to do since the days of Carb.io is assess the fit of market *segments*. When I worked on a startup called Athlon, doing this helped us find our best market segment, which was not the one we had first aimed at. The key tool we used was the product funnel.

I use the product funnel as a "meta funnel" to measure the strength of PMF across markets, needs, and solutions. I started using this funnel to track my customer development process when I was struggling to articulate why one segment felt better than another. We only had subjective data, collected from our interviews, and we found that our personal opinions were working their way into the conversations as facts. I had already tracked every person I talk to in a big CRM-like sheet so it wasn't too hard to add in a few extra columns. The hardest part was filling it out and keeping it up to date.

Here are the stages:

1 **Acquisition:** When you tell them about it, are people excited to talk about it?

2 **Activation:** Do they actually sign up / pay / follow through on your call to action?

3 **Retention:** When they sign up, do they keep using the product?

4 **Referral:** If they use it, was it so great that they tell their friends?

Some of you may have noticed these are Dave McClure's Pirate Metrics, minus the revenue step.[18] I'm intentionally leaving revenue out because I start measuring these stats when I'm pre-revenue and usually pre-product. This evolves as the product goes from nothing to something, and I want to be able to compare the same metric between pre- and post-revenue products. It's not a perfect model because there are some problem spaces where referrals are not natural or allowed. If this is the case for you, revenue is a fine proxy.

It's super important to tag your users by different variables when you're exploring. With Athlon, a product we launched to

---

18  Dave McClure, "Startup Metrics for Pirates," August 8, 2007, slideshare.net/slideshow/startup-metrics-for-pirates-long-version/89026.

help people build healthy fitness habits, we had 15 characteristics that we tracked under the user profile, 10 for the reason they exercised, and one Ideal Customer Profile (ICP)/Persona category.[19] When you filter your funnel by different variables, it helps you identify trends you might miss when looking at the broader audience. When we first started working on Athlon, we thought we'd focus on semi-pro athletes, but we also interviewed some random friends of ours just to build a wide sample. What we found, as the clickbait headlines say, shocked us.

In our data spreadsheet, we logged each person's name, answers to their profile and context questions, pain questions and ratings, and any relevant notes. The best part of putting it all together in a spreadsheet is you can sort and filter. When we took our Athlon interview data and sorted the sheet by people we thought matched the semi-pro athlete category, we noticed that their collective scores were significantly lower than those of casual users. I'm sure we could have put together some fancy stats and graphs, but we didn't need to. Filtering by customer persona, reason for exercising, and problem statements was good enough to point us in the right direction.

When we looked at the data, it was pretty mediocre. But there was a cohort of folks that, when we filtered by only their data, had really high scores. They were people who used to play sports or work out four to five times a week but were struggling to regain the habit after having kids. Many of them were exercising because they wanted to get back to a previously lower weight. I belonged to this group, but it was my buddy Karl, who also belonged to the cohort, who gave it the name "fat dads." It started out as a bit of a joke, but the data backed up that it was a pretty interesting niche.

---

19   ICP is that "business soulmate" you're convinced is your perfect match—right up until data swoops in with a plot twist.

Here are my customer development interview stats for Athlon:

**Total conversations: 47**

Conversations are Stage Zero in my funnel. Everyone I talk to starts here. Only when they meet the entry criteria of the next stage do they get moved to it. If you follow this model, make sure you and everyone you're working with are using the stages in the same way.

Step one of finding people to talk to is telling the people you know about the problem space you're trying to solve. Part of doing this well is being able to communicate your first two hypotheses, market and need, very succinctly. When asking for intros or referrals, leave your solution out of it. Instead of telling the person about what your product does, tell them about the people you want to serve and the unmet needs you think they have.

When there are big unmet needs in a market, people are usually quick to whinge about it. If you can't find anyone who complains about why X is so hard or Y doesn't make sense, you need to look at either the problem you're solving or the way you talk about it.

**Acquisition: 38 (81 percent)**

At the end of every customer development interaction, I like to have an ask. We are trying to quantify momentum, and having an ask at the end gives us a measurable next step. In the early days, it might be booking a follow-up interview once you have a little more built out. Once you have something built, it might be an ask to try out the software. When the thing is closer to its final state, I start asking for money. The trick with that is to be generous but not silly. If the product is 5 percent complete, I ask for 5 percent of what the final price will be. This helps you understand if people are willing to pay and if they have any objections about how you're thinking about pricing the product.

For Athlon, roughly 80 percent said yes. What I learned from the other 20 percent was that most of them belonged to an ICP that didn't care about the problem we wanted to solve.

### Activation: 26 (68 percent)

Great products get used. I've had many people tell me they'd "love to try" my CRM only to completely ghost me after I sent over their demo credentials. Here's another dirty sales secret of mine: If you're going to offer to let someone demo your software, book a meeting with them for a week later to see how it's going. This will tell you if they are excited about using it and, if they did use it, how their experience was.

I don't care if your product is B2C, free, or only for werewolves. If you're not booking a feedback call after they've tried out your product, you are leaving information on the table.

For Athlon, 38 people said they'd be interested in checking it out (acquisition). I sent them an invite to try the platform. This is where the rubber met the road, because it is much easier to say yes to a hypothetical offer than a real one. For Athlon, the activation numbers weren't so great, in my opinion—only 26 people actually clicked the link and signed up.

### Retention: 10 (38 percent)

After people sign up, do they actually use the product? Entrepreneur Mark Roberge has some great thoughts on finding leading indicators of customer success, and I highly recommend checking out his excellent post on the science of scaling.[20] The most important piece is that your product delivers on your promise to solve their unmet need well enough that people keep using it.

---

20 Mark Roberge, "The Science of Scaling," Stage 2 Capital, stage2.capital/science-of-scaling.

Once people were live on the platform for Athlon, I wanted to see how many actually continued to use the product. This is where we ran into trouble. We ended up retaining 38 percent of the activations. It was an indication that our product wasn't amazing yet, which we knew because it was super early. As people exited the funnel, I would reach out to book interviews with them so I could understand why they dropped off.

**Referral: 9 (90 percent)**
Great products that solve large unmet needs tend to be so exciting that their users feel a need to tell everyone they know. Tracking the referrals you get from each customer was the best proxy measurement for excitement I could find. It's objective and reinforces something you should be focusing on anyway: making people so happy that they tell their friends. I mostly cared about two numbers: the percentage of people we talked to who referred us to another user, and how long it took to go from first conversation to first referral.

The reason this is the primary focus is that the people you do customer development interviews with should be your first customers. Your next customers are very likely to come from referrals from the first ones. If I'm not able to walk someone from first conversation to referral, it is a strong indication that growth will be challenging. It doesn't mean I don't have a product or a market to sell it to, it's just that the market isn't pulling my product from me very strongly. I'm trying to measure that pull.

The thing that surprised me the most with Athlon was the referrals. Of the 10 people who ended up using the platform, almost all of them referred us to at least one more prospect to talk to. This was a really strong indication that we had found something interesting.

Alas, while we did find that people had the pain we thought existed, we couldn't find a way to create a real business around it. The users were consumers, but we wanted to pursue a B2B model selling to employers and couldn't find a good way in. Our team of three ended up running out of steam and we went our separate ways. There's probably still an opportunity there, we just weren't able to make progress on it given the time and resource constraints we had.

Our total funnel efficiency was 9/47, or 19 percent, from conversation to referral, which in hindsight is pretty strong. It took us an average of 30 days to move someone from conversation to referral, which isn't as great.

Your numbers will be different and that's OK. The reason to represent this as a funnel is it tells you where you need to focus if you want to make things better. For Athlon, I could see that we were losing most of our customers at the retention stage. That told me that while we had something interesting, our tool needed to be better if we wanted users to onboard unassisted.

Sometimes the market just pulls the product out of you. In those situations, the rate of conversion to referral doesn't accurately represent the full strength of your product-market fit and you need to add a time variable into the mix. A funnel that converts to referral in seven days is significantly better than one that takes 30 days to accomplish the same feat. Here is the formula I've used to calculate my Product-Market Fit Strength:

PMFS = Conversation to referral rate × (1 ÷ Time)[21] × 1,000

If I compare the scores of Athlon, the startup we worked on for 14 months and never made any revenue from, with Carb.io, our startup that scaled from $0 to $1 million in a few months, it's pretty clear from the formula that one is better than the other.

---

21  Time = number of days from conversation to referral.

> Athlon strength of PMF = 0.19 × 0.033 × 1,000 = 6.27
>
> Carb.io strength of PMF = 0.40 × 0.14 × 1,000 = 56

These scores are snapshots from a specific time period, so they're only useful as a way of comparing the two startups. This is just a proxy I use when I'm comparing projects that I'm considering. Be careful when you compare your score to someone else's. If there's one thing I've learned from helping fix sales teams, it's that everyone uses their stage definitions a little differently.

## The MarketFit Process

One of the toughest lessons I've learned (and the reason I'm hammering so hard on documenting product-market fit) comes from my days running an outbound agency. Time and time again, I'd see founders who *did* find product-market fit—but never fully documented or shared what they'd learned. They'd hire a sales leader, fail to pass along all the crucial insights about ideal customers and messaging, and then get frustrated when campaigns flopped. We'd build sequences and lists based on incomplete information, only for the sales leader to say the leads "weren't right." That frustration built up so frequently that we built MarketFit.

The MarketFit process breaks down everything we've learned about finding and validating market fit into three testable hypotheses: targeting, need, and solution. Think of these as the three big questions you need to answer: Who are we trying to reach? What do they want? How can we help them? This process will help transform a hypothetical ICP into a tangible set of criteria and segments your sales team can run with.

This process might feel like skipping ahead but it's important to start documenting things now while they're fresh in your memory. This process is an excellent way to communicate your product-market fit with precision.

Let's break each hypothesis down.

### The Targeting Hypothesis

This is where most companies start—and where most go wrong. They look at surface-level traits like industry and company size, build a list, and start selling. But effective targeting goes deeper. You need three layers:

First, there's the company profile (what most people call firmographics). This includes the usual suspects: industry, employee count, revenue, location. But here's the key—you want to prioritize characteristics you can actually search for in data providers. We call these "searchable" attributes. There's no point building your ICP around attributes you can't find.

Next comes the persona. Who in these companies are you trying to reach? This goes beyond just job titles. You need to understand their level (director, VP, C-suite), their function (sales, marketing, product), and their department. Again, focus on what you can actually search for.

Finally, there are behavioral signals—things that indicate a company or person might be ready to buy. This could be recent funding, conference attendance, technology usage, or website activity. These are harder to track systematically but can be gold when you find them. Tools like Clay.com and Apollo.io are particularly powerful here. For how-to guides, go to tools.terrifyingart.com.

### The Need Hypothesis

This is where we dig into what your target market actually wants. It combines several key elements:

**Persona responsibilities** are what the person was actually hired to do. The easiest way to figure this out? Check job postings for their role. These responsibilities create the foundation for understanding what drives their decision-making. For a sales leader, this might include "build and manage a high-performing sales team" or "develop and execute sales strategies."

**Goals** are their annual objectives—the concrete outcomes they're measured against. These aren't abstract aspirations; they're the specific targets they need to hit. For a sales leader, this might be "increase revenue by 50 percent" or "build a predictable pipeline generating $2 million in new business."

**Jobs to be done (JTBD)** are the specific tasks they need to complete to achieve those goals. Think of these as the "how" behind the "what" of their goals. If their goal is to increase revenue by 50 percent, their JTBD might include "invite potential customers to sales calls" or "maintain a steady flow of qualified leads."

**Obstacles** are what's getting in their way. What's making these jobs harder than they should be? What friction points exist in their current process? This might be "manual prospecting takes too long" or "can't find enough qualified leads."

### The Solution Hypothesis

This is where you connect what you offer to what they need. The solution hypothesis has four key components that work together to create a compelling narrative:

**A unique and believable solution:** Strip away the marketing-speak. Describe in plain language exactly how you'll solve their specific problem. No jargon, no buzzwords—just the simple truth about how you can help. Your prospects can smell marketing fluff from a mile away, so keep it real.

**Position in the market:** If it's relevant for this specific prospect, explain how you're different from competitors. Don't try to be all things to all people—focus on what makes you uniquely valuable for this particular situation. Sometimes this isn't relevant, and that's OK. Only include it if it genuinely matters.

**Proven results/Social proof:** Let your happy customers do the talking. Use their actual words to describe the impact you've had. Even better, include how they quantified that impact. Real results from real customers are worth their weight in gold. "We increased our qualified pipeline by 47 percent in the first three months" beats generic testimonials every time.

**Relevant trends:** Identify current market or industry developments that make your solution more compelling right now. These trends can make your chain of relevance (which I'll discuss next) more urgent or important to your prospects. For example, if you're selling an AI-powered sales tool, relevant trends might include "the rise of remote selling" or "increasing pressure to do more with smaller teams."

## The Chain of Relevance

Each link needs to connect logically to the next. When it does, you've got a compelling story that resonates with prospects because it matches their reality. This provides the context for your message but is not the actual message that you'll send—that comes later.

### Mapping Out the Chain of Relevance

| Targeting Hypothesis | | | Messaging Hypothesis | | | |
|---|---|---|---|---|---|---|
| Company | Persona | Responsibility | Goal | Job to Be Done | Obstacles or Friction | Product or Service |

Need Hypothesis spans from Responsibility through Obstacles or Friction.

### Testing Your Hypotheses

Here's where your hypothetical ideas meet reality. For each combination you want to test, you need at least 300 prospects. Why 300? Because that's the minimum sample size you need to get statistically significant results.

Start with your targeting hypothesis. Can you actually find 300 prospects that match your criteria? If not, your targeting might be too narrow—or you might need to broaden your search criteria.

Then test your need hypothesis. Are these prospects actually responding to messaging about the goals and obstacles you've identified? If not, you might have the wrong need hypothesis.

Finally, test your solution hypothesis. When you connect with prospects, does your solution resonate? Do they see how it helps them achieve their goals? If not, you might need to rethink how you're positioning your solution.

### Getting Started with Messaging

When you're staring at a blank page trying to write your first message, it can be overwhelming. It's tempting to go hunting for templates, but resist that urge. Instead, try this approach: Focus on just one element of your chain at a time.

You could start with:

- **Goals:** "Are you trying to hit that 50% growth target this year?"

- **Obstacles:** "Is manual prospecting eating up too much of your team's time?"

- **JTBD:** "How are you keeping your sales pipeline consistently full?"

It could also be any other element that feels natural. Test different starting points and see what resonates. Almost anything is worth testing when you're just getting started. The key is to start somewhere and iterate based on the responses you get.

Remember, this is an iterative process. You'll probably need to test multiple combinations before you find one that works. But when you do find one that works—when you see prospects consistently engaging with your message and moving through your pipeline—you'll know you've found a profitable segment of your market.

The key is to document everything. Track what works and what doesn't. Share the learnings with your team. And most importantly, keep refining your hypotheses based on what you learn from the market.

**Resources for Going Deeper**

To help you implement this process, we've created two resources for this book:

- **The MarketFit Process Spreadsheet:** a template for documenting and tracking your hypotheses, chains, and results
- **Kenny MacKenzie's MarketFit Training Course:** a detailed walkthrough of how to implement every aspect of this process

These tools will help you put everything we've covered into practice. The spreadsheet gives you a structured way to document your work, while Kenny's course provides detailed guidance for each step of the process. You can access them at terrifyingart.com/resources.

## Asking for Money

The act of handing over money is what turns a stranger into a customer. The whole point of doing customer development interviews is to find unmet needs. The first test of whether your buyer thinks those unmet needs are worth solving is whether they're willing to pay for a shitty first version of your product. And you'll only find out if you ask them. To misquote Wayne Gretzky, "You miss 100 percent of the sales you don't ask for." Even if your product isn't ready to be used yet, you still need an ask.

I don't remember the first person we interviewed specifically for the Carb.io software platform. We started by offering it as a service and built out the software from there. We interviewed plenty of customers, but they were predominantly exploratory interviews. When it came to building the software, we had an internal team of five people who were prospecting on behalf of customers using Gmail, Google Sheets, and a mail merge script I had copy-pasted from various sources. We were able to sit down with them regularly, see where they got stuck, and see where they didn't realize they were missing things.

When we launched the service that turned into Carb.io we had the advantage of having recently interviewed 50 sales leaders, so we had a pretty good sense of where the gap was. We skipped right to Focused Customer Development Calls. My goal going into them was to see if people cared enough about solving sales development rep (SDR) productivity that they would pay me to do it manually. I figured I'd try to recruit some people who were just interested in paying me some money to solve the problem regardless of what the solution looked like. I interviewed friendly entrepreneurs who I thought might care about growth or improving the performance of their SDR teams. Every interview process was interrupted with a question like "Are you really thinking of solving this?" My first interview ended with the prospect asking what I could do for $500 a month and introducing me to two other people he knew were struggling with this problem as well. They bought from me too.

I offered the first five people I interviewed a manual solution to their problem for $500 a month, just for one month, to see if it worked. I ended up with seven customers from those five interviews. I had found a sizable and important pain and my offer was priced low enough to make it a no-brainer for people who felt it, and high enough to filter out anyone who didn't really care.[22]

I priced my service offer at 10 percent of what I thought it would cost them to solve it manually themselves. Because it was manual I couldn't afford to do it for free. Plus, I wanted a strong signal that this was something worth pursuing. After the first round of customers, I doubled my price after every round. The $500 was a strong yes, and $5,000 was an eventual yes but took much longer. For $500 I acted as an SDR for the customer for a month but used email only. It was a Wizard of Oz beta and I was the man behind the curtain—hence the ability to only take on seven clients for a month.

Not every problem can be solved Wizard of Oz–style, so I'll leave it up to you to find a way to get a commitment. Here are a few ideas I've tried, and I'd encourage you to play around with some of your own:

- **Wizard of Oz beta:** Nothing exists yet, so we'll do it manually.
- **Use it for free, tell me what you think:** You're not expecting real adoption and are just looking for feedback.

---

22 Contrast this with my customer development process for voltageCRM: I never had an offer and I spent 18 months working on something only one customer purchased.

- **Future commitment—if I build this, will you use it?:** They commit to using it once you have X, Y, and Z features and put up a deposit.
- **Prepaid design partner:** They commit to using, paying, and providing feedback.

Your offer will depend on where your product is at. The most important piece is that you ask the people you are interviewing for some money. Don't be too excited when people say yes or too sad when they say no—you are collecting another data point. If someone tells me that their pain is 10/10 importance and 2/10 satisfaction but declines my offer, I know I need to ask more questions. I could have the wrong persona (they might be too low in the organization), they could have just been acting polite, or there might be an organizational complexity that I haven't understood yet. Either way, the offer acts as a check to make sure I'm not progressing through my interviews with false assumptions.

As a salesperson or leader, I hate discounting but I do make an exception for alpha and beta pricing because the solution isn't 100 percent complete. The revenue you get from the offer isn't likely to be significant; the primary value will be learning and future referrals.

No matter what, do not give people "free forever" deals. If people want to use it, let them know that it's free during alpha and will then have a gradually increasing price as you build out more features. It is totally OK to give your first few customers a great deal and let them keep early pricing. Just make sure you are very clear about your intentions. I knew I couldn't sustain my Wizard of Oz beta for Carb.io, especially at $500 a month, so I was very clear that it would only last a month.

You are graduating from learning to selling full-time, so throw yourself a party, because that was hard work. The work you put into finding a number one pain and creating something that is 10x better is going to make everything you need to do afterward, which we'll explore in the following chapters, so much easier. A product that solves problems for people who are struggling to solve them already nearly sells itself. *Nearly.* You also have some selling to do. Ready?

# FIVE

# HOW TO SELL

**Change is the essential process

of all existence.**

MR. SPOCK[23]

**'VE SOLD USED CAR.** Not "cars," just one. (Don't worry, I'm not contagious.) I took the job because my mom told me not to and I'm a terrible son. She was right, I hated it, and I quit two weeks later after only selling one car.

Selling cars is a hard game. You spend most of your time waiting for someone to walk in. When someone does, you glance around the room to see if you're "up," and then you're in action. That's if people at your dealership follow the "up" system—some don't. The "up" system is a rotation between the reps that gives everyone about the same number of people to talk to every day. It's easy to see how this environment leads to undesirable customer experiences. When a large part of your paycheck relies on commission, and you have no ability to impact the number of leads you get, *and* you don't know when you'll have another shot at closing a deal, you tend to push each lead a little bit harder than prospects might like.

So it's clear that I didn't make my fortune selling cars, but selling voltageCRM was even harder. People at least needed to buy the cars that were on our lot. voltageCRM was like selling a car that was great for the kids in the back but a terrible ride

---

23  *Star Trek: The Original Series*, season 3, episode 15, "Let That Be Your Last Battlefield," aired January 10, 1969, on NBC.

for everyone else. Nobody asked for it and nobody wanted it, but I pushed hard to find customers for it anyway. Contrast that experience with Carb.io, where I felt like I had the golden sales touch. My sales abilities didn't matter one bit because everyone was so excited about the progress that Carb.io would help them make. Prospects were showing up to the calls having already decided to buy. My mentor Lars Nilsson calls this the Paper Problem: "In my day, strong product-market fit was keeping enough paper in the fax machine to keep up with the orders coming in." This checks out with my experience selling Carb.io. All I needed was the sales skills of the kid working the drive-through at McDonald's. Prospects found me and were hungry for a solution, and I was just there to take their order. When your PMF is strong the sales call is just a victory lap that allows prospects to feel like they did their due diligence.

Selling directly to consumers sucks, at least in my experience. People can be irrational and emotional when spending their own money (myself especially!). It takes a special type of human to be able to absorb all their energy and try to help. I don't have it in me. I strongly prefer selling to other businesses. The same people who make irrational and emotional purchase decisions as consumers are much easier to work with when someone else's money is on the line. This removes most of the emotion from the equation and lets us focus on solving problems.

Selling to businesses is about helping them make progress on something important to their bottom line. You have three ways you can help: increase revenue, decrease costs, or reduce risk. Remember that first impressions are important, and if you start off a relationship as the person who helps them decrease cost, eventually the only way to get their cost lower will be to push your price (and commission) down. On the flip side, if you're the person who helps them grow revenue, they'll always look to you when they have money to invest in more growth. Take Predictable Revenue's consulting business as an example. We provide everything a team needs to get a sales development team up and running (sales dev leader, sales ops, tools, data, etc.). When we talk to a customer, we could lead with cost savings ("it's cheaper than building internally") or revenue generation. Either one could work in theory, but 99 percent of people care about increasing revenue.

If you are a founder, you are in sales. It's OK, you'll be fine. Most people base their opinion of the sales profession on their personal buying experiences, which are not usually positive. It's frustrating when you can tell a salesperson is doing something just because they want the commission. It feels like they're only pretending to care about your problems so that they can find a way to extract the highest commissions from you. With experiences like that, I can see why people would be hesitant to jump into the sales seat. But fear not, this is not how most salespeople are. These bad encounters are not the norm, and when it comes to B2B selling, making a sale is more like solving a riddle than playing some emotional game.

In this chapter, I'm going to help you see why you don't need to be afraid of sales. It doesn't matter if you come from engineering, product, or broccoli farming. I'll walk you through everything you need to be great at sales and share why you're probably already the best rep your company will ever see. There are no magic tricks, special hand signals, or secret midnight meetings. Learning to sell is like learning another programming language: At first, you'll struggle to understand the structure and logic because it feels unnatural, and your "code" (sales conversations) might not work as intended. But as you practice, debug your mistakes (review your calls), and get feedback (deals close or not), you will start to see patterns and refine your approach. Over time, you'll create a cleaner, more effective "program" (sales process) that consistently delivers the desired results. Just like coding, selling is about breaking problems into manageable parts and finding solutions that fit.

And here's a bonus: if you've already done customer development interviews—and you should have—you'll find the sales process I lay out to be very similar to the one for interviews. You probably already know how to do 80 percent of the sales process, so I'll walk you through the last few pieces you'll need to know. Many founders struggle with sales because their misconceptions about selling get in the way. I'll use this chapter to clear up some of those misconceptions and lay out what a good sales process looks like.

## Stop Treating Prospects as Something You Need to Close

When I first got into sales I thought there were magic words or phrases that would help me improve my ability to close customers. I remember reading a wide range of books, from sales to fringe psychology books, to find that edge. What I was missing was that people buy when they have an unmet need they would like to solve. Nothing I say will be able to change the reality of their situation.

It took me some trial and error, testing stupid ideas on prospects. I remember trying a silly closing tactic on a customer—fortunately it was over the phone—and he called me out on it. Essentially it was like asking for the trophy before the tournament started. I did not get the sale, but I did get a verbal ass-kicking. I had lost sight of the fact that my prospects were people and I was treating them as a way to get my commission check.

Eventually I realized the importance of valuing customers for their own sake, rather than using them merely as a means to an end. When this happened, my perspective shifted from trying to maximize my commission check to maximizing the number of people I could help. This shift helped me put less emphasis on getting prospects to the outcome that earned me money. I now focused on helping them solve their problems, regardless of whether it was with our solution. I saw myself as a critical part of the customer's decision-making process. My role was to help them make a good decision by using my knowledge of the problem space that our product lived in. The quality of the prospect's decision now mattered to me more than the outcome.

I once worked with a founder named Gordon and remember him talking about how he couldn't wait to get a "real salesperson" in the door. Then I asked about their last three years of sales performance, which was pretty decent. I reminded him that he was the number one sales rep (on a team of one) at his company for the last three years and asked how he expected someone new to come in and outperform him so quickly. He thought that anyone with sales experience would be able to do that. What do you think? Who is likely to be a better salesperson (initially at least), the person who understands the problem better than anyone else in the world, or the person who knows how to spell BANT?[24]

The purpose of building a new company is to help a future buyer solve a problem they couldn't solve before. Sales is just a small step on the buyer's journey from problem identified to problem solved. As a founder, you're the person who went

---

[24] I'm not trying to take anything away from the complexity or professionalism of the sales craft. I've always seen sales as my trade and likely always will. My goal here is to help founders see that they already have the skills and knowledge to help buyers solve their problems, so sales will actually be much easier than they think. Also, BANT stands for Budget, Authority, Need, and Timeline and is a common method for communicating how qualified a prospect or opportunity might be.

through the customer development interviews, heard firsthand about people's unmet needs, and built something to address the gap in the market. Nobody will be able to relate to your future customers better than you can. A salesperson's advantage would come from having a good process and being able to deliver it confidently. I can guarantee that prospects would rather talk to someone who deeply understands the problem they're facing than someone who knows how to run a tight sales call. Your delivery won't be perfect, and that's OK—it'll be authentic. Showing people that you care deeply about helping them make progress on something important to them is enough to make up for any sales process pieces you miss.

Immanuel Kant, the philosopher, argued that rational human beings ought to be viewed as an end in their own right, rather than as tools for achieving other aims.[25] We need to think of our customers with the same respect. We are in the business of creating successful customers, not merely making them successful as a means of growing our company. Sales and GTM are just ways of scaling up your ability to help people.

## The Myth of Great Sales Teams

I used to believe a great sales team could solve any growth problem. That somehow, no matter what the competitive landscape looked like or how dire the financial backdrop was, truly great sales teams could find a way to get deals done. When I started the company that became Predictable Revenue, I thought that we'd be able to help any company grow. Back in 2016, I still hadn't figured out why some of our customers took off

---

25  Immanuel Kant, *Grounding for the Metaphysics of Morals*, 3rd edition, translated by James Ellington (1785; reprinted by Hackett, 1993), 30.

like rocket ships while others languished. Until a new customer shattered my belief in great sales teams.

In December 2015, Uber signed on as a client, preparing to launch Uber Eats with the goal of going live with the top restaurants in all major US cities at once. They tasked our team with reaching out to target accounts and setting appointments for their reps to meet with restaurant owners. You're probably familiar with them by now, but their offer to restaurant owners at the time was akin to "we'll save you money and bring you more customers." Backed by Uber's highly recognizable brand, we were very confident that this campaign would go well.

At the time we had an incredible account strategist, Krista Caldwell. She was responsible for booking 10 meetings a month for each of her clients. She outperformed everyone else on the team despite using a Bluetooth mouse to click around on her phone. She regularly put up 60 meetings a month across an average of five clients, which was top of her class. When Uber signed on we decided to move all of Krista's clients to someone else so that she could focus 100 percent of her efforts on them. We kicked off the campaign in the first week of January and by the end of the month she had booked 327 meetings for them. My. Head. Exploded.

I remember looking at our stats for these campaigns and not being able to understand the sheer volume of replies and meetings that were coming out of so few emails. It was taking Krista most of her day just to get back to all the positive replies, book meetings, and make intros to the appropriate rep. At the time, our benchmark was a 3 percent positive reply rate and a 1 percent meeting booking rate. Somehow, this client was getting 37 percent and 33 percent. This meant she had just booked 327 meetings after reaching out to a little under 1,000 accounts. We were stunned. It made sense that Uber's campaign would do well, but we never expected to see rates like these.

How much credit should Krista get for the campaign's success? She worked hard and made smart decisions. If she repeated the 37 percent positive reply rate with another client, she deserved full credit. But even if she couldn't, she still did a great job. We couldn't replicate this success with other clients, which shows that Uber's strong product-market fit was the key factor in their 5x increase in meeting output.

Uber eventually left, thanked us for our help, and hired 100 business development representatives to replace us. While the temporary bump in revenue was very nice, what we learned was even more valuable.

The experience showed us two things. First, product-market fit isn't all-or-nothing; it's somewhere on a scale from weak to strong. Second, product-market fit acts as a multiplier of your sales efforts. Uber got a 33x multiplier on our service because they had such strong PMF. To see what I mean, look at the table below. It shows two hypothetical clients managed by Krista: she gave a 100 percent performance for both clients and her role's impact on the situation is 1. Client A has a Product-Market Fit Strength of 50 and Client B's is just 1. Krista is going to put the same quality and effort level into each one, but Client A will receive 250 meetings and Client B will get 5. This is the impact we have seen firsthand running tens of thousands of sales development campaigns, sequences, and plays.

|  | Krista's Performance | Impact of Krista's Role | Client's Strength of PMF | Impact of Client's Strength of PMF | Monthly Meetings |
|---|---|---|---|---|---|
| **Client A** | 100% | 1 | 50 | 10 | 250 |
| **Client B** | 100% | 1 | 1 | 10 | 5 |

## The Anatomy of a Sale

There is no secret trick or tactic we can use to convince someone who isn't in pain to suddenly spend thousands of dollars. What we have are the questions we ask (the information we learn), the stories we tell, and the information we share—in other words, our process—and the people involved and how well trained they are. Everything else is outside of our control. By knowing and accepting the difference, we can focus our attention on the right things.

If you want to be a great salesperson, there are four things that you need to do: find unmet needs, build a business case, influence how the prospect thinks about the decision criteria, and don't drop the ball.

**Find unmet needs:**
1 If there are no unmet needs, there's no progress to make and nothing to sell.

2 A strong discovery process will maximize your probability of finding unmet needs.

3 Your goal is to understand the shape of their problem and make sure it aligns with the shape of your solution.

**Build the business case for solving them:**
1 Identify the situation and relevant context.

2 Make a diagnosis—define the nature of the problem.

3 Give a recommendation—make a business case for solving the problem.

4 Take action.

**Influence how the prospect thinks about the key decision criteria:**
1. Find out if you're up against "do nothing," do-it-yourself, or a competitor.

2. Know the radar graphs of your alternatives (strengths/weaknesses).

3. Share stories, metrics, and case studies that highlight why your unique attributes make your business a better solution to their problem.

**Don't drop the ball:**
1. Book next steps—schedule the next step while you're still on the call. (The next step is always a next call, even if it's just to check in on progress and offer some free advice.)

2. Maintain a high do:say ratio (do what you say you will at the time you said you'd do it).

3. Be open and honest about the shape of your solution and the results you can drive.

4. Know where you're really at by using shared definitions and qualification methodology (more on these in chapter 8).

A great sales conversation is, first and foremost, a conversation. But it is not an emotionally charged, high-pressure interaction—it is a coming together of equal parties with different knowledge to exchange ideas and decide if it'll be profitable to work together. That goes both ways.

The four-step process for building a business case—situation, diagnosis, recommendation, and action—is called the Selling V, and I have adapted it from something I learned from my college professor, Chamkaur Cheema. He taught much-feared sales courses that required students to "sell" scholarships to the college to local businesses. Some people hated it, but I loved it.

There is nothing like being forced to get real-world sales experience to wake up a drowsy student brain. I have added some ideas to his method that I learned from Richard P. Rumelt's book, *Good Strategy/Bad Strategy*, as well as things I've picked up from various podcast guests. Let's break the process down.

### Situation

Your prospect's situation provides the relevant context, and your goal is to understand it. Here are some ways to approach this:

- **Context:** What relevant context do I need to know?
- **Progress:** What is the progress they're looking to make?
- **Metric:** How does the prospect quantify the impact of making the progress? What is the cost of doing nothing? What are the benefits, costs, and risks associated with each option?
- **Summarize the situation:** Do I understand correctly?

### Diagnosis

The diagnosis defines the nature of the problem. This involves looking at what you know about their situation to find the reason behind the problem. This isn't about placing blame—it's about getting to the core of the issue so that you know what you're trying to solve with your prospect. Sometimes there are multiple pains and it's important to discuss all the alternative diagnoses to make sure you arrive at the root cause of the problem, not a symptom. It goes basically like this:

1 **Define:** What is the nature of their challenge?
a) What is it that caused this problem?
b) What is the pain?
c) What is the root of the pain?

2 **Summarize the diagnosis:** Does the prospect agree with it?

Getting to the point of mutual understanding requires multiple steps of summarizing and confirming. The first comes at the end of the situation stage when you summarize what you've heard and ask what you've missed. Once the prospect agrees that you understand the context and haven't missed anything, you can move on to the next stage. The second summarize-and-confirm comes at the end of the diagnose step. This is where you have discussed the diagnosis and the prospect agrees you have found the root cause. Now that you understand their side and they know that you understand, you've unlocked the ability to talk—just a little—about your solution. This is where the similarities with our customer development process end and we enter sales territory. With customer development interviews, your goal was to understand the prospect's situation, but now that you have something to offer, the prospect needs to understand your situation as well.

**Recommendation**

The recommendation makes the business case for solving the problem. It's where you define how you think your solution could solve the root of their problem and help them realize the benefits they are looking for. Most recommendations will center on using your solution, but not all of them will. There will be prospects that aren't a fit for your solution, and your best move is to recommend they go in a different direction. Recommending a client away has two benefits: It demonstrates to the prospect that you honestly care about helping them solve their problem; and sometimes we misunderstand something and get the recommendation wrong, and this gives prospects a reason to tell you why you are wrong and they really are a good fit for your product.

The recommendation stage follows these steps:

1 **Explore:** Lay out all the potential paths forward to see which one appeals the most to the prospect.

2. **Educate:** Make sure they understand the strengths, weaknesses, and risks of each path forward.

3. **Recommend:** Make a recommendation based on your experience and what you've learned about them so far. A good recommendation summarizes the progress you'll help them make, why your company is uniquely positioned to solve the pain, and the outcome they'll realize.

4. **Solicit feedback:** Ask them to try on the recommendation to see how it fits.

Once you've made your recommendation, there are two ways the conversation can go: either the prospect will lean in and start asking questions (you have a live one) or they'll try to wind down the conversation (you've missed something). The recommendation stage ends when you present the business case and the prospect understands it and agrees with your logic.

## Action

Your action plan communicates how your solution will work for your prospect. This is where you may want to show a quick demonstration of a feature or a few slides with visuals explaining a complex idea. It's also where the prospect is going to ask about the most relevant parts for them. I like to lay out the high-level steps and let the prospects direct the conversation to where they feel they have gaps.

Here's a totally not real example:

- **Situation:** I was roughhousing with my brother, swung my arm at him, and hit the door. It hurts.

- **Diagnosis:** The bone has a hairline fracture.

- **Recommendation:** Stop playing hockey and cast it for six weeks.

- **Action:** Apply a plaster cast, wait six weeks, tell the patient not to pick at it, and reapply the cast two weeks later because he picked it off.

When you approach your customer conversations in this manner, you're not trying to sell them something. You are asking questions that will help determine if there is a justifiable business case for working together. It's not an emotional process—it's a logical exercise that helps you understand all the variables that will go into the spreadsheet.

## Sales Philosophy

One of my first B2B sales roles was assigned to me because I'd found a way to automate my marketing role by copy-pasting a few macros from Stack Overflow together. I was asked to follow up on some leads to sell the Evacutrac, a portable wheelchair evacuation device, to churches and community centers. These are for any public building that needs a way of evacuating someone in an emergency when the elevators are shut down. The leads were old and I was struggling to get anywhere with my calls, so Mike Morisset, our top rep, sat me down to give me some advice.

"Imagine yourself in a wheelchair on the third floor of our building," he said. "A fire has just broken out and all the elevators are shut down. How are you supposed to get out?"

I paused, stuck in the hypothetical nightmare.

"That's what you're calling for," he said. "It's not about the money. Your goal is to help that person get out of the burning building."

Suddenly, the cold list of leads didn't seem so scary.

If you're worried about taking on the sales role, reframe it by thinking about the impact your product has on the end user and their business. How does it impact their bottom line, the goals of the person who made the purchase, and all the people who might be affected either directly or indirectly? If your product is genuinely helping people solve problems, you are on the cusp of acting maliciously if you don't do your best to find everyone who might share the problem. I love solving problems, and sales conversations are especially fun when you're helping someone make progress on something that's important to them.

Our role in sales is to support our customers in making a buying decision. Our commitment to our prospects is to be open and honest, not to use high-pressure sales tactics. Yes, we will try to exert some influence over how they see things, but that's our job. Yes, we acknowledge that we're a little bit biased, but we make an honest effort to stay neutral. We salespeople are experts in helping prospects make decisions in our problem space. Sometimes those decisions will go our way, and sometimes the right thing is to point them in a different direction. If we want customers to trust us, we must have the integrity to tell them when the business case doesn't support working together.

If you want to help the prospect make a good decision, you need to have a good process for understanding all of the variables. As salespeople, we must know two things extremely well: one, the problem space, including all of the variables and alternatives; and two, the decision-making process—how to weigh the upsides and downsides of the alternatives so that the prospect can make the right decision for themselves. If they choose to work with you, that's a bonus. Our commitment as salespeople is to the process, to helping our prospects make a great decision, regardless of the outcome of that decision.

I'm reminded of something written by Annie Duke, the author of *How to Decide* and *Thinking in Bets*: "Your goal is to be an expert decision-maker, not an expert outcomes collector." I find this idea helps sales reps detach their self-worth from the outcomes they collect. You're a great salesperson if you consistently follow a great sales process. It's an overattachment to the outcome that gives people "commission breath," leads to a reliance on discounting, and creates a culture where high-pressure tactics become the norm. There are a few organizations in the sales tech space that have decent tools but that I refuse to work with because they have a horrible sales culture. I won't name them here, but you definitely won't find me recommending their stuff.

Giving yourself and your reps permission to detach from the outcomes doesn't mean doing away with forecasts, quotas, or performance expectations. You need to plan for all eventualities, and that includes deals slipping at the last minute. But you also need to keep the long view in sight. I remember a conversation I had with a sales rep where we ended up going down a philosophy-of-sales rabbit hole. There were 10 days left in the month, he had missed quota the previous month, and I could tell he was wound up pretty tightly, so I asked him to share. He was super stressed because it was getting close to the end of the month, he was about 70 percent to target, and he had deals in hand but was angry because a couple of big ones weren't going to buy this month.

"Tell me about why you're frustrated that those deals pushed to next month," I said.

"It means I'm going to miss quota this month," the rep said, slightly tensing up. He was clearly fearing the repercussions.

"And?" I shrugged.

"And I really don't want to let the team down." Implying me.

"Fair enough," I said. "Did the deals go away?"

"No, they just weren't ready yet."

"How come?"

"They didn't have the bandwidth to implement."

"But they're in for next month?"

"Yeah." I could clearly see the relief in his body language.

"So," I said, "the only thing that we lost was getting them started this month?"

"Yeah."

"OK, so we didn't lose the deal, we just took a revenue hit this month that we'll make up next month?"

"Yeah."

"So the only thing we got wrong was the timing?"

"Yeah."

"Is that really that bad?"

"No," he replied after a pause, coming to the realization that yes, it sucks to miss quota, but it doesn't mean the world is coming to an end.[26]

Customers will buy when they're ready to make a change, and you need to be OK with that. My conversation with the rep eventually drifted back to philosophy. I shared the Annie Duke quote about not being an expert outcomes collector and told him that her words reminded me of the Stoics. He was less familiar with their work, so I laid out their three core tenets:

- Control your perceptions.
- Direct your actions accordingly.
- Willingly accept what is outside your control.

I repeat these words to myself as a mantra any time I feel like I'm on tilt and need to calm myself down. Here's what they mean to me in a sales context.

---

26  Dear friendly sales leader reading this section: You're right. In a well-built sales organization, with all the supporting processes, teams, and technology, this would be a problem. But I'm writing specifically for founders at an early stage when none of that exists. I'm also speaking to founders who still own the sales process, which means they have two or three jobs worth of work to do. Having a deal push at this stage isn't worth losing sleep over.

## Control Your Perceptions

The Stoic philosopher Epictetus, in his *Enchiridion*, wrote, "Men are disturbed not by things, but by the views which they take of things."[27] Being emotional is something we do to ourselves, not something that is done to us. Yes, our body has automatic reactions to things and that's OK. But we have the power to choose how we feel about a situation. It is not an easy thing to learn to do, but with practice, it is possible.

The rep was mad that the customer pushed to the next month. He let the fact that a customer wasn't ready injure them. When he reframed his role as master of the process instead of an outcomes collector, he was able to see that interaction in a new light. We still did a great job of serving the customer, which is the most important part. When we took the emotion out of it, instead of being mad at the customer for pushing, we were able to find a gap in the rep's process that led to the miss and coach him on how to do it better for the next customer.

It's about the process, not the outcome. Good process will lead to good outcomes.

## Direct Your Actions Accordingly

Epictetus also wrote, "First, say to yourself what you would be; and then do what you have to do."[28] It's easy to say that we want to have a sales process that is so loaded with value that prospects should pay for it, but it's another thing to actually make it

---

27 *Enchiridion* 5, from Epictetus, *The Works of Epictetus: His Discourses, in Four Books, the Enchiridion, and Fragments*, translated by Thomas Wentworth Higginson (Thomas Nelson and Sons, 1890), perseus.tufts.edu/hopper/text?doc=Perseus%3Atext%3A1999.01.0237%3Atext%3Denc%3Achapter%3D5.

28 Epictetus, *Discourses*, Book III, ch. 23, § 1, perseus.tufts.edu/hopper/text?doc=Perseus%3Atext%3A1999.01.0237%3Atext%3Ddisc%3Abook%3D3%3Achapter%3D23.

happen. It's also easy to say that the process is more important than the outcome. It's another thing to live it in how we forecast our quarters, work with customers, and push back on growth targets that would require compromising on our commitment to the customer.

How this fits into my mental loop is that I make sure I am seeing a situation clearly and not adding any bias or emotion to it. Then I ask myself what reputation I would like to have or my team to have. Then I make a decision that serves my reputation goal. It's not always the easy decision. In fact, it's usually the hard thing to do. Every decision is an opportunity for me to vote with my actions—do I want to be the salesperson, leader, or human that I aspire to be, or do I want to be someone who takes the easy path? The more ticks I have on the right side of the equation, the closer I get to living in accordance with my goals.

### Willingly Accept What Is Outside of Your Control

In *Enchiridion* Epictetus wrote, "Some things are up to us and some are not. Our opinions are up to us, and our impulses, desires, aversions—in short, whatever is our own doing. Our bodies are not up to us, nor are our possessions, our reputations, or our public offices, or, that is, whatever is not our own doing."[29] In other words, we cannot choose our external circumstances, but we can always choose how we respond to them.

This is my favorite part of the loop, and it's also the hardest. Our process, team members, and technology are within our control. Whether a prospect goes on holidays, has a different priority, or doesn't like the color of something is outside of our control. This tenet is the most freeing for me, because it gives

---

29  Epictetus, *Enchiridion* 1.1, *Handbook of Epictetus,* translated by Nicholas White (Hackett, 1983).

me permission to not beat myself up about things I can't control, but it was the hardest for me to implement. I didn't realize how accustomed I had grown to putting the blame for my failures on things outside my control. When I look back with this lens, it helps me see with clarity what I need to do next time if I don't want to repeat that mistake. Without this framing, this book would be filled with useless excuses and wouldn't be helpful to anyone.

When I'm doing a pipeline review or talking about deal strategy, this is the lens that gives us the most power. It helps us cut through the noise and focus our attention on what we can control. Sometimes there's nothing and we have to learn to accept that. If we miss our forecast, I can choose to be angry about it or not. I'm certainly not perfect in this regard—growing a company can be an emotional sport. But now, when we miss or have an issue, I'm sometimes able to let that first wave pass and keep our attention on what is within our power. This helps me keep myself and the team leaning in the right direction.

I'll never forget a conversation I had with my good friend Megan Wilson, a seasoned enterprise seller who's navigated some of the most complex deals out there. We were talking about a deal that I was confident would close, and she hit me with a question I hadn't considered: "What's the risk? What could stop your deal from progressing?" Megan has spent most of her life working large, complex deals and always seems a step ahead in any deal she's working. Why? She takes the time to consider the risks and then actively works to mitigate them. Risks can range from small things like someone critical to the buying process going on holidays to potential deal killers like your champion leaving the company. The point Megan drove home was that every deal has risks—no matter how sure you feel. The key is to identify them early and plan for how to navigate or mitigate each one.

And in many ways, that's Megan's own application of Stoic thinking. Rather than lament the things outside her sphere of influence—like a holiday schedule or sudden budget changes—she focuses on the areas she can control: uncovering risks ahead of time, rallying the right stakeholders, and setting clear next steps. When you're knee-deep in deal complexity—multiple stakeholders, heavy competition, shifting timelines—it's the risks you didn't see coming that have the potential to derail months of work. By refusing to ignore even the smallest hazards, Megan stays one step ahead—and that focus on the controllable aspects of the deal is exactly what empowers her to close some of the most challenging opportunities.

# SALES HABITS

If I had five minutes to chop down a tree,

I'd spend the first three sharpening my axe.

NOT ABRAHAM LINCOLN[30]

**G**REAT SALESPEOPLE aren't special. They just consistently do a lot of little things right.

I remember seeing someone presenting a demo of Domo at Dreamforce back in 2014 and walking away thinking, "This is the best sales rep I've ever seen." The product looked incredible, it would answer all of my data and dashboarding problems, and it was well out of my price range. (He also gave me a free pair of Skullcandy headphones just for watching the demo, so that didn't hurt.) Here's a question for you: How much credit does that rep deserve for delivering such an excellent demo?

The answer will depend on a few things, like who created the process, how much training he received, and who helped him practice. Did he create their demo script, or was that a team effort? How did he learn the script? Was he trained by a team or did he figure it out solo? Did he have a sales leader coaching him and providing feedback? Did he have colleagues who were also contributing to improving the demo process based on their experience? And we still haven't touched on the product, which

---

30 The origin of this quote, which has often been attributed to Abraham Lincoln, is not entirely certain, but it definitely wasn't honest Abe. More likely Rev. W.H. Alexander of Oklahoma City. See quoteinvestigator.com/2014/03/29/sharp-axe.

was beautiful and functional—a rarity in enterprise software at the time.

I'm not trying to take any credit away from the rep; he clearly put the work in and did an excellent job. The point of these questions is that this salesperson was successful because of a number of factors. There are some salespeople who are just excellent on their own, but they are extremely rare. Most great salespeople come from great sales organizations. And great sales organizations are created by founders who understand that sales is a team sport.

This chapter will cover some sales habits that have served me throughout my sales career. I can't take credit for creating any of them—they are things I learned from different sales leaders, podcast guests, and mentors along the way. Before I get into the habits, it's important to call out that reading them will only go so far. You'll need to practice, try them on real calls, and get feedback from someone you trust on how well you did. I have been selling for nearly 20 years and I still ask for feedback after a call.

To start with, I want to talk about buckets. You know, the things that hold water, ice cream, and lists of things we want to do before we die. If your bucket is in good shape and you have a steady hand, it can help you transfer its contents from one place to another. However, if your bucket is in bad shape—maybe it's a bit rusty and has a few holes—it will be less effective. See where I'm going here? You're the bucket. If you're going to be stepping into the selling role, *and you should*, then it makes sense to invest in filling any holes before you start trying to carry anything.

I was working with a founder—let's call him Paul—and he wanted to work on his pitch. He had built a pretty interesting product in a well-defined niche but wasn't closing as many deals as he would have liked. I knew it wasn't going to be a perfect call when he insisted on pulling out his slide deck two minutes into it.

Personally, I hate sales decks. Professionally, I understand there are occasionally times when they can be helpful, but the biggest reason slide decks ruin a sales conversation for me is that they are pre-built. The reason to involve a salesperson in a sales process is to provide a bespoke buying experience. Of course reps should have a defined process, but that process should involve tailoring the conversation to a buyer's unique circumstances. Presenting a long-form sales deck gives the buyer the same content experience as watching a YouTube video without the ability to skip ahead or change the playback speed. It's frustrating and I'm very likely to turn my video off and start ~~clipping my toenails~~ answering emails. Same with demo'ing your product. If your product can solve my problem, I don't care what color it is.

When you share your screen, whether it's a demo or a deck, you're splitting your prospect's attention between your visuals and what you're saying. There is a time and a place for this; some products have a magical "aha" moment worth illustrating or require a visual to explain a complex idea. But if you are going to share your screen, keep it to just the one point and then get back to talking to them. If you have multiple things to show, kill your screenshare between each one and the next.

I can almost hear you shouting, "If I'm not demo'ing my product, what am I supposed to do?" Great question, I'm glad you asked.

The best part of talking to a great salesperson is the bespoke buying experience. A great salesperson has a deep understanding of the problem space, asks questions to understand your circumstances, and uses that information to make an informed recommendation. Great salespeople are catalysts that help buyers accelerate a change they want to see in their business. Catalysts can only increase the rate of a change that is already taking place. If you want to be a catalyst, you need to start by asking questions to find the reactions that are already bubbling.

There is always change happening in an organization—no CEO, founder, or shareholder is ever happy with the status quo. Your job is to find the change they want to make and see if it aligns with what your product can do.

Recommendations are how salespeople create change. You're not saying, "Here, buy my shit," you're handing them a shirt and saying, "Try this on and let me know what you think." It's a directional question, not a closing tactic. You're saying to the prospect, "Here's what I see and how I think I'd solve it—what do you think?" You're just sharing an idea and asking for feedback. The best part of this process is it prevents you from going down the rabbit hole of talking about features and benefits of products that the buyer doesn't care about. You're basing what you're going to talk about next on how they see the problem.

When you reframe sales to make it about helping buyers solve problems, the actual sale is the smallest piece. A great B2B sales process is really just the onboarding details for how a prospect makes progress on this big, hard problem they have. Good salespeople don't manufacture problems or convince prospects to solve something in a way that doesn't make sense. They simply help them understand the shape of the problem and find out if it'll be well served by the shape of the solution.

Making a change in a business is not something people do for fun. Change usually starts with someone noticing that something is broken or could be much better. First they need to diagnose the root cause of the issue—is it a people, process, or technology issue? It could be one, two, or all three of them. Once they've diagnosed the issue, they need to figure out the best way to solve it: better process or people, more people, or a piece of software or a service to fill a gap. Then they need to find a tool that closely aligns with the shape of their particular problem and make the business case internally that they should purchase it. Next, they buy and implement the tool. Reaching the magical "problem solved" moment can take one to 12 months depending on the problem's complexity. After three months, their team is likely to have adjusted to the new tool and process. After six months they're probably close to full adoption.

In most cases, the actual dollar cost of your product or solution will have the smallest impact on the customer. The internal cost of the implementation usually outweighs the amount spent on the actual software licenses. Implementation costs include configuring the software, changing internal processes, and retraining staff. But even these are just first-order costs. The second-order cost is the time it takes, from a "did I hit my goal this quarter?" perspective. So when you're selling to businesses, it's not like selling a shirt, where they give you money and you give them a shirt. You're guiding them to a solution that will take an investment of time to resolve their pain and produce the sought-after value. You're like a trainer giving them a fitness program to do, and you need to approach the interaction with the whole process in mind.

## Getting "Do Nothing" Off the Table

The last step in closing a deal is overcoming the inertia of doing nothing. Making a change in an organization means more work and political risk. If your champion is going to take on that risk, they're going to need to understand why their company will lose X in profit for each day they hesitate to pull the trigger.

Once we got Paul to stop whipping his deck out at the beginning of every call, his pipeline started to grow, but deals still weren't closing. He asked me, "What's the best path when urgency isn't there? During the sales process the initiative got deprioritized." The most likely answer is that the project was never really a priority, but he assumed it was.

He likely assumed it was a priority because the call was pleasant and the prospect liked the way the software looked. But he didn't ask good questions that would have helped us understand the prospect's situation, the progress they wanted to make, and the impact solving it would have on their organization. They were still considering doing nothing, but we didn't know it.

So how do we get "do nothing" off the table? Well, we can and we can't. Good discovery helps you uncover if "do nothing" is off the table, and it will only be off the table if the ratio of value creation to value capture is high.

First we have to draw a distinction between what is under our control and what is not. Let's start with what is under our control:

- the rep who shows up to the call
- the skills training the rep has received
- the process the rep has been taught
- the technology that supports the rep and process

Now, let's look at what is outside of our control:

- the prospect's annual and quarterly priorities
- their company's priorities, goals, and financials
- the priorities of the other people at our prospect's company who are also trying to do things that will improve the bottom line

This does not mean we can blame our lack of success on things outside of our control. By understanding what's inside and outside our control, we can pinpoint where we invest our time so that we can do better next time. The goal of discovery is to determine whether there's a strong business case that can be made for moving forward with our solution. If there is, we should book next steps. If there is not, we should share our perspective with the prospect, see if they agree, and recommend another solution.

The biggest piece that was likely missed in this case is the process: Paul just didn't ask the right questions that would help us uncover a strong business case to be made for moving forward with our solution. The prospect either didn't have the budget in the first place or was competing for a slice of his boss's budget and a coworker had a project with a higher expected value.

If you understand the appropriate context about a deal, the progress they want to make, and the impact that progress will have on the organization (more profit or less risk), then you should be able to build a rough model that calculates the return on investment (ROI). If you can't do this, you probably haven't asked good enough questions.

While Paul had managed to build a decent pipeline, most of his deals were stalling out at the pricing stage. There are two reasons why this happens:

- There is not enough ROI to justify investment (out of your control).
- You didn't find a critical factor in proving the business case (in your control).

For clarity, in the first example there was not enough value creation to justify moving forward. In the second example, there was enough value creation, you just didn't ask the right questions to uncover the answer. If you want to avoid deals stalling, start having honest conversations with prospects about whether they should do anything. Don't be afraid to inform them of better options—it's the right thing to do and it demonstrates your integrity.

## Stop Answering the Question, "What Can You Do for Me?"

One of the best ways to screw up a sales conversation is by answering the "so tell me what you can do for me" question at the top of a call. It's painful to admit I had to learn this one a few times, from a few different people.

When I was first coming out of customer development mode with Carb.io and finally getting to sell something, all I wanted to do was talk about the thing we were finally building. I remember one of my mentors, Howard Olsen, listening to me on a sales call one day. We were a minute into the call when he sat back and started shaking his head. He smiled and said, "Catch and release." The prospect had asked me about the problem we were solving and I launched into pitch mode, talking about the research we did and the gaps we found. While my delivery was pretty good, my timing was very poor. I spent the next six minutes on a tangent about everything I knew about what was wrong with sales development, and then the prospect checked out. We did not get the deal.

Prospects don't care about what you do until they know you understand their problem and believe you might be able to help. It's not that the information you're sharing is bad—it's probably great, it's just the wrong time to share. When you're talking you're not learning.

I'll say this again: The reason humans get involved in a sales process is to have a tailored buying experience. When you "show up and throw up," you might as well be a prerecorded video. No judgment if you're doing or have done this—I've probably done it more than you have. But the next time a prospect says, "So tell me what you can do for me," say what Howard Olsen told me to say:

"I'd be happy to—do you mind if I ask you a few questions first?"

Feel free to make the language your own. The most important part is to judo-flip the conversation from talking about you to getting them to talk about themselves. Most people want to talk about themselves, their company, and their product anyway.

## Stop Sending Follow-Up Emails

If I told you that a 30-second habit could save you 30 minutes on every deal you work, would you be interested? I bet you would.

There's nothing worse than having a great sales call, thinking "I've got a real one here," and then not hearing anything back. You wait a week, then think "they're probably just busy," so you go back through your notes and start composing the perfect email. Thirty minutes later you've hit send, checked your email twice, and still crickets. Are they busy? On holidays? Is this not a priority? You don't know because you didn't try to book the next step. Next time you're coming to the end of a call, instead of saying goodbye and running off to the next one, pull out your calendar and book your next call together. It's simple, but there is some nuance to it: The next call needs to be framed in a way that makes it easy to say yes to.

Just 30 seconds of trying this approach will save you 30 minutes of agonizing over how and when to send the perfect follow-up email—I know because I've been there too. The only time I won't set next steps is when I have confirmed that there is no chance our two companies can *ever* work together. If that's the case, let's not waste each other's time. If it's not the case, we're setting next steps before I get off that call.[31]

---

31  Sales manager side note: When I'm reviewing a rep's pipeline and see a late-stage deal with no next call booked, I almost immediately write it off. It might not be dead but it sure doesn't look healthy.

Working a deal is like swinging from the monkey bars: Momentum is everything. As we're moving to the end of the call I will recap our next steps, mention that when I have these conversations people usually have questions afterward, and then ask how their calendar looks in three or four business days. For clarity, I'll actually say the names of the days. If I have any days that are fully booked or holiday time I'll be sure to call them out. It sounds a little like this:

"Great getting to know you all today. For next steps, I'll send those links I mentioned and, Sarah, I have a note for you to talk to Jane about that process and get back to us. Did I miss anything? Great! I find people usually have questions after these conversations, so how about we grab some time together next week. I'm traveling Monday, but how does your Tuesday look?"

Notice that my "next week" sentence ends in a period. While it might look like a question, I say it like a statement and then ask the calendar question right after it. You can ask them both as questions, but I find I get the same result when I do it this way, and this way is faster, which can be important at the end of a call.

One of a few things will happen next:

- 70% of people will agree and open up their calendars.
- 20% will push back and ask you to send something first.
- 10% won't agree.

Not only do you save yourself the follow-up work but you also learn something about where you really stand in the deal. Bonus points if you ask whether there's anyone else they should add to the next call. This helps you get other decision-makers involved in the process early. The 70 percent who agree right away are the ones most likely to move forward with you. Congrats, you just saved yourself and your prospect a bunch of time emailing back and forth.

For the 20 percent who push back, you've learned something. Either they don't think it's a top priority or they have a super busy calendar for the next few weeks. If their calendar is hectic, it's OK to schedule something a few weeks out. Think about what would have happened if you hadn't asked: You would have left the call thinking it went well, followed up a few times when the prospect was busy, and thought you lost the deal because they never replied.

Now is not always the right time for a company or individual to solve the problem you can help with. It's OK to be respectful about your buyer's journey. If I'm talking to a prospect and the timing isn't right for them this quarter, I'll still book a next meeting, but it'll be in three months. The most important piece of setting a meeting like this is to understand what needs to change between now and then for the conversation to make sense. When you understand this, you can send much more impactful follow-up emails. When you schedule a meeting that's a few months out, it's a good idea to drop the prospect an email a few days ahead of time to see if now is the right time. If it is, great. If not, I'll move the meeting further back. This is a good example of nurturing a prospect, and I'll dive deeper into related tactics and processes in chapter 8.

For the 10 percent of people who won't take a call, they either have no intention of buying from you or they are difficult to work with. Either way, this filters out people who are only going to waste your time.

## Set Next Actions and Dates for Every Deal

Back in my day, CRM was something that a salesperson bought and installed on their computer. It was my personal productivity tool and if bossman wanted a live view into my pipeline, they had to walk over to my desk and take a look or figure out how to sync the SQL server on my laptop to their shared drive. Many tried but few succeeded (at least with my machine). Setting up the CRM was my responsibility and I took ownership of making it work for me. Tools like Maximizer, Act!, and GoldMine were as common as Word back then—even my grandfather, a retired real estate agent, ran Act! If you don't believe me, go ask any salesperson over the age of 40.

When Salesforce brought CRM to the cloud, we salespeople suffered a dramatic loss of productivity and control. We no longer could define our own process and stages and instead had to adapt our process to whatever our sales manager or Salesforce consultant decided was best. This was a huge loss in productivity and autonomy for us. If you're a manager and wondering why CRM adoption and utilization sucks, this is why. Your system was optimized to provide the dashboards and reports that you and the execs needed, but this can come at the expense of the reps' productivity. Just imagine if I came and took whatever productivity tool you currently use, dictated that you needed to change your process, and then made you use a web application that requires numerous page refreshes to create a new task. In 2012, I counted the number of page refreshes it took me to create an opportunity with a new contact in Salesforce, and it was 17.

Now, as someone who has been using Salesforce since 2005 and built their own CRM (RIP voltageCRM in 2013), I clearly don't believe that modern CRM is bad. It's actually great but usually just badly set up. Rep productivity is rarely something that I've seen considered when digging into people's CRMs. Most salespeople either use their sales pipeline as a to-do list or have a process outside the CRM for keeping track of what they need to do next. Any productivity tools that your reps use that are outside your CRM represent a process leak that will eventually pull their system of management from your CRM and into whatever tool it is. Our goal as sales leaders should be to patch all these process leaks by making it easier to do tasks in the CRM than somewhere else.

The solution to this problem is two simple fields added to your Opportunity/Deal object:

- **Next Action:** a plain text field containing what the rep will do next to move the deal forward
- **Next Action Date:** when that action needs to occur[32]

Bonus tip for reps: The number one productivity tip I can give you is to fill out these two fields as close to immediately after each customer interaction as possible. The reason it's so effective is that you have all the relevant context loaded into your memory, and thinking through what needs to happen next will take a short time. If you don't do this, your brain needs to work through all the relevant context every time you look at an opportunity in your pipeline. This not only takes a long time but also increases the risk you will forget something. If you do this on every customer interaction for two weeks I promise it'll save you so much time.

Bonus tip for managers: There are only three fields in my CRM that I make sure my reps always keep up to date: Next Action, Next Action Date, and Opportunity Stage. I also don't have any required fields[33] because, on average, they slow down

---

[32] Shout-out to David Allen's *Getting Things Done* (Penguin Books, 2015) for the original idea and Ryan Reisert's buckets system for reminding me of this amazing idea.

[33] I'm referencing Salesforce's "Required Fields" setting here, where you can't create a new object or save an existing one without completing the field. They are destroyers of a sales rep's flow and tend to be put in place to make up for a lack of training and onboarding for sales teams. Strong sales organizations don't need Required Fields because their reps actively use the important ones. Is this an overreaction to past Salesforce admin trauma? Almost definitely but I'll never admit it.

rep productivity and increase the risk of getting inaccurate data. These three fields, in conjunction with objective definitions for your funnel stages, will tell you everything you need to know about where each deal is at.

My favorite part of David Allen's book *Getting Things Done* was the idea of Mind Like Water: "A mental and emotional state in which your head is clear, able to create and respond freely, unencumbered with distractions and split focus." When you have a system of organization that you trust, your brain gives your subconscious permission to forget about all the deals you're working on. The hardest part of sales, especially for founders who are new to it, is that they don't have a great organization system.

I have Next Action and Next Action Date on every opportunity in my CRM. Every day, I sort my pipeline by date (today at the top) and work my way down the list. The beautiful part of this is I don't need to load every opportunity into my mental RAM to figure out the best use of my time to move my deals forward. Every day I look at the top three or four opps I need to follow my own advice on. I am one with my habits and my habits are one with me.

You don't even need a CRM to keep track of next steps on opportunities—a spreadsheet works just as well, especially if there's only one of you. We offer a template that's free and requires very little setup. Grab a copy of it at terrifyingart.com/resources.

## Start Recording Your Calls

Recording and listening to your calls is one of the most awkward experiences. It's also one of the best things you can do to improve your sales habits. It took me years to get over the cringe of listening to my own voice, but it's worth it. When you review your calls, you'll catch the little details you missed during the heat of the conversation—things the prospect said that you glossed over, opportunities you didn't jump on, or questions you wish you'd thought to ask. You'll also start to see how your prospect reacts to your pitch. Were they leaning in and engaging, or did they check out when you started explaining a key point? Did your pitch land the way you thought it did, or was it off the mark?

At the end of the call, their energy is another huge indicator. Were they excited to book a next step, or were they counting the seconds until they could hang up? These moments tell you a lot about how the call went and how well you're building momentum. And here's the bonus: Your recordings aren't just for looking back. They're amazing prep tools for looking ahead. Before you hop on the next video call with the same prospect, rewatch the last few minutes of your previous one. It's the perfect way to remind yourself of where you left off, plan your next move, and match the energy of the previous call.

Be brave. These calls aren't just for you to review—get your mentors, cofounders, and anyone else with sales experience to give you feedback. The openness will help you identify gaps in your process that you might be missing. I've been selling for over 20 years and I still ask for feedback on calls. I might be good but I can always get better.

## What Comes Next

Eventually, you'll reach the point where you need to build out your first real go-to-market channel—maybe that's launching outbound sales or spinning up a content engine—and you'll want to bring on your first sales hires. Before you do that, though, you have to lay the groundwork with simple, repeatable processes and by making sure you are already following the best practices you'll want to teach to your new hires.

In the next chapter, we'll zoom out from these individual habits and look at the four main funnels that drive growth. This foundation of solid routines will help you make the jump from founder-led sales to a structured revenue engine that scales well beyond you.

## SEVEN

# HOW TO BUILD YOUR FIRST CHANNEL

**Never half-ass two things.**

**Whole-ass one thing.**

RON SWANSON, *Parks and Recreation*[34]

JUST BEFORE Carb.io took off, I remember sitting at my laptop one day and staring at a revenue forecast and wondering where the hell we were going to find all the prospects to help us achieve these numbers. All of our customers up to that point had come from our network or referrals from existing customers. While it was exciting, it wasn't the rocket-ship growth that I'd hoped for. Then, one week, Aaron Ross mentioned us in his Predictable Revenue newsletter and our growth really kicked into high gear. Aaron had built a huge following, so his recommendation carried significant weight. There was also hardly any information on tooling out there, so the audience was ripe for the information.

Aaron wasn't the first influencer I had reached out to. I found a list of 50 sales influencers and contacted all of them, interviewing about 20, but none of them were interested in what we were doing. I was offering to build their methodology into our CRM and let them resell it to their audience. I thought it would have been extremely interesting to them. Alas, I was wrong again. When I initially reached out to Aaron, it was for advice. He had written a book about cold email and, being a

---

34 *Parks and Recreation*, "Ron Tells Leslie 'Never Half-Ass Two Things' | Parks and Recreation," November 12, 2019, video, 1:15, youtu.be/k6hz9KdG1QU?si=mfA2-yJASICES-aH&T=40.

good Canadian, I figured it would almost be rude not to email him with a quick question. Slowly, our relationship turned from advice-seeking to knowledge-sharing. We found a way for him to monetize his reach in a way he couldn't before. Eventually, Aaron approached us about the idea of merging our software company with his consulting firm, and Predictable Revenue was born—and still thrives today. But that's leaping ahead a bit.

Most people reading this chapter won't have a newsletter, a thought leader, or a big brand to rely on. I'll admit that in this part of my startup journey, I definitely felt like I was cheating. Doors opened easily and customers seemed to fall from the sky. Part of it was the strength of the product-market fit, but finding someone like Aaron to partner with was like finding the Konami Code—that's geek speak for a secret button combination for early video games that gave you some combination of bonus lives and special powers. Is it really cheating if it's part of the game? I'm not saying you should cheat, do anything illegal, or pin your hopes and dreams on a single influencer. However, if you can find an individual or organization that can help you quickly scale up your reach, in my experience it's worth it. Just be aware that we were extremely lucky and that most partnerships don't work out for startups, especially for finding your first customers. If you can't, don't stress—it's time to start building your audience and reputation.

Once we got the Predictable Revenue rocket boost, it seemed like we were on an infinitely scalable journey. In reality, we were at the base of a curve that looks like this:

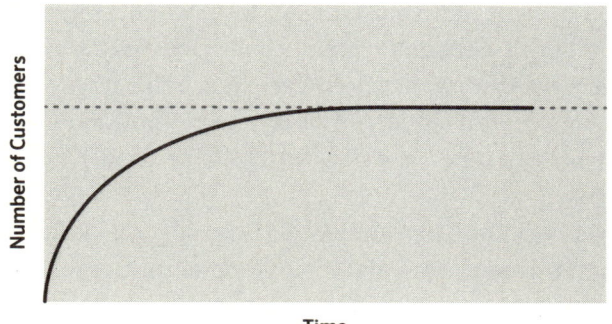

It's important to realize the mechanics of demand generation channels so that you're not surprised when growth slows and you're stuck at another plateau. In hindsight, we could have done some very basic math to model out this curve. But we didn't. And we were surprised when growth plateaued.

Aaron's newsletter helped us get off the ground, but it was the webinars, partner newsletters, and speaking that really expanded our reach. We knew this, but when we looked at our analytics, the lead source was almost always the newsletter or people typing "predictable revenue" directly into their browser. In reality, it was the power of Aaron's book *Predictable Revenue* and the reach that its success had given us that was really driving things. All of our marketing activities were aligned with supporting the reach of the book.

## What You Need to Know Before Investing in a New Channel

Before building your product, you need to think about channels. I know it sounds backwards—shouldn't you figure out the product first? Yes, but here's the thing: The channels you choose will have a huge impact on whether you can profitably reach your customers. Even the best product in the world will fail if you can't connect with your audience in a cost-effective way. At the core of this decision is price. Your price point will determine whether your product fits a freemium, product-led growth pattern or sales-led motion. In turn, your revenue motion will shape which channels are likely to work profitably for your business.

When I was starting Carb.io, this was the piece of the business model canvas that made the least sense to me. I kept wondering, "If I haven't built the product yet, how can I know which channels will work?" The answer, it turned out, was about making sure we were building our product in a way that would align with our revenue motion. Freemium and product-led growth rely on low-friction channels where users can self-serve, meaning the product must be simple to adopt and deliver immediate value. By contrast, a sales-led motion supports higher price points but depends on costlier channels like outbound sales or events.

Another key consideration is whether you're selling B2B or B2C. This distinction shapes nearly every aspect of your go-to-market (GTM) strategy, from sales cycles to decision-makers and channels. B2B sales typically involve longer cycles and multiple decision-makers, requiring high-touch motions like direct sales or account-based marketing. In contrast, B2C strategies often focus on reaching a broad audience quickly, favoring scalable channels like social media, influencer marketing, or paid search.

The complexity of your product also plays a significant role in determining the right channels. Straightforward products, which are easy to understand and adopt, can thrive in self-serve models with low-touch channels. However, complex offerings that require customization, training, or a deeper understanding of a client's needs often demand high-touch channels like partnerships or direct sales to deliver the necessary level of interaction and support. By aligning your channels with your price point, target audience, and product complexity, you set the foundation for a GTM strategy that works.

If you did your homework in Focused Customer Development and asked the people you interviewed how they discover tools similar to the product you're building, you're golden. If you didn't, it's time to go back to the interview step. Go back to your customers and the people you interviewed who didn't buy and ask them how they typically find and buy products in your space. Then make a list of all the channels they mention, sort by frequency, and start working out ways of testing each one.

## The Founder's Role in Building a New Channel

I was having a conversation with a new client, Matt Wyman, the cofounder of Okareo, who said something that immediately caught my attention: "I want to prove it myself, then I'll bring in someone to scale it." That's exactly the mindset most founders need—but don't always have—when launching a new channel. Matt understood the principle that only the founder can pull off the tricky early-stage work of validating a channel. And once the core assumptions are proven out, *then* you bring in someone else to optimize and scale.

Why does this matter so much? There are a few reasons:

**Founders have unique leverage.** In early stages, the founder typically has unparalleled product knowledge and the ability to cut through bureaucracy or skepticism. As Paul Graham's essay "Founder Mode" argues, founders can do things—like skipping levels in the org chart and making decisions on the fly—that a hired manager can't.[35] Matt recognized that no one else on his

---

35  Paul Graham, "Founder Mode," September 2024, paulgraham.com/foundermode.html.

team could move as quickly or with as much conviction to validate a new channel.

**Prove it, then scale it.** Like Matt, I strongly believe the founder should personally run initial experiments, talk to potential customers, and confirm that a channel can be profitable. Once the data shows promise, that's the time to hire a growth marketer or sales lead to take the process you've developed and multiply it. Skipping straight to "hand it off" is a recipe for confusion—and often for failure.

**Founder mode vs. manager mode.** Conventional "manager mode" wisdom says hire great people, set KPIs, and step back. But when it comes to building brand-new channels, stepping back too soon can kill momentum. Matt's approach was more in line with "founder mode," where you lead from the front, iterate quickly, and course-correct in real time. You can't always do that effectively when you're relying on secondhand reports.

**Stay close to the learning loop.** Early GTM experiments are full of subtle insights—discovering new pain points, refining your pitch, seeing which audiences respond best. Founders who stay hands-on in these initial phases pick up a wealth of knowledge that no one else can easily replicate. You'll be able to train and guide your future hires much more effectively because you've *lived* the process.

Matt Wyman's "prove it first" mentality was a refreshing reminder of what I wish more founders would do. Don't delegate the hardest part—the front-end proof of concept—until you, as the founder, have iterated enough to see it working. Once you hit that threshold, you can bring in specialists to focus on fine-tuning, scaling, and optimizing. That's the moment where your role evolves from *proving* the channel to empowering others to scale it.

## Four Paths to New Customers

When you break it down, there are only four ways to grow your business. Every growth strategy, no matter how complex it seems, will fit into one of these categories: referrals, upsell/expansion, earned, and paid. Each has its own strengths, and the real challenge is figuring out when to lean into each one.

- **Referrals:** Your product is so great, people tell their friends.

- **Upsell/Expansion:** Your product is so great, customers buy more from you.

- **Earned:** Things you do work and get a result, like organic social, SEO, and outbound.

- **Paid:** You cultivate a market through paying money for things: ads, events, sponsorships.

Let's start with referrals. This is growth in its purest form—people who use your product can't help but tell their friends. This kind of growth is the most valuable because it's organic, carries built-in trust, and costs you almost nothing. But it's also unpredictable. Referrals can come in waves, so you can't rely on them to always be consistent. That's why you need a plan to encourage them, whether that's a referral program, incentives, or simply asking satisfied customers to spread the word.

Next is upsell/expansion. When your product is so good that customers can't get enough, they'll naturally buy more from you. Maybe it's upgrading to a higher tier, expanding into new features, or bringing your solution into other teams or departments within their organization. Upsell and expansion are critical because you've already done the hardest part—acquiring the customer. Now it's about maximizing the value of that relationship. To succeed here, you need to understand when and how to offer more without coming across as pushy.

Then there's earned growth. These are the things you do that work and get results without spending directly on ads. This could be organic social media (free messaging, such as posts), SEO, or outbound sales efforts. Earned growth is powerful because, once you get it working, it scales without eating into your budget. But here's the catch: It takes time and effort to build up. You need consistent, valuable content, strong SEO practices, and a disciplined approach to outbound outreach. But when earned growth clicks, it has a compounding effect, delivering returns for the long haul.

Finally, there's paid growth. This is where you put money behind your efforts, whether it's ads, events, sponsorships, or anything else that requires a budget. The biggest benefit here is speed—you can turn it on, get in front of your audience immediately, and see fast results. But there's a downside: Once you stop spending, the growth stops too. Paid channels can be a great way to accelerate your growth, especially when you need quick wins or want to scale up fast, but you've got to watch your customer acquisition cost (CAC) and make sure the numbers stay in line.

These four ways to grow aren't standalone tactics—they're levers you can pull at different times based on what your business needs. The key is understanding when to use each one and how to balance them to create sustainable, profitable growth. Referrals are great, but you can't wait around for them. Upsell and expansion are critical, but they depend on your customers' needs. Earned growth builds momentum, but it takes time. Paid growth gets results quickly, but it requires budget and close monitoring. Unfortunately, there are no magic beans or silver bullets. The trick is finding which channel will provide the outcome you're looking for. If you do believe in magic beans, this link will *definitely* solve all of your problems: magicbeans.terrifyingart.com.

## The Stages of a New Channel

When you start working with a new channel, there are four stages you'll need to go through. Ramping a channel isn't about throwing money at it and hoping it works. Instead, you're testing, optimizing, and scaling it in stages. Each stage tells you something about the channel and whether it's worth further investment.

Sizing your experiments correctly can have a massive impact on whether your tests produce meaningful data. For example, if you spin up a sales development rep (SDR) team, only give them a few months of runway, and expect to see closed deals, you're going to be disappointed. It takes 12 months for a team to find their footing and 24 before the numbers start to get really good. It's the biggest reason why many founders have had a bad experience with any channel: They didn't realize there was a minimum buy-in to get a full picture. It's like sitting down at a $10 minimum blackjack table with only $10—unless you are extremely lucky, your night will be over before it even starts. If you don't want to rely on luck for ramping a new channel, I recommend following these four stages.

The first stage is Proof of Life. Your goal here is simple: Show that there's something interesting happening. You're not trying to scale yet—you just need proof that this channel can bring in customers. This is the phase where you run small experiments to see if there's even a pulse. If you're running ads, you're testing copy, audiences, and offers. If it's cold outreach, you're testing different messaging and seeing how people respond. The goal isn't to be perfect; it's to get a sign that there's potential. If you can get a few meetings booked, a handful of sign-ups, or even just strong engagement, you've passed this stage.

Once you know there's something there, it's time to Optimize. Now you take what you've learned from those early tests and make the channel better. If you saw engagement with certain messaging, refine it. If you had some ads that performed well, start tweaking the audience and get creative to boost performance. This is where you're squeezing out as much efficiency as you can. You want to see conversion rates go up, costs go down, and overall performance improve. Optimization isn't a one-time thing—it's an ongoing process of testing and tweaking until you've built a well-oiled machine.

Next comes Profit. This is where the rubber meets the road. You've proven there's life, you've shown that you can improve things, and now you need to show that the channel can be scaled profitably. At this stage, you're increasing your spend or volume to see if it can still perform as it grows. Can you continue to get customers at an acceptable cost? Can you keep your CAC in check as you scale? If you've done your homework in the optimization phase, you should start to see some real returns here.

The final stage is Double Down. Once a channel is profitable at scale, you step on the gas and scale aggressively. This is where you pour resources into the channel until you hit a point of diminishing returns. As long as the numbers make sense and the CAC remains under control, you keep investing. But be careful—every channel has its limits. You need to keep a close eye on performance to know when it's time to pull back or shift focus to another channel. The key is to keep pushing until the channel starts to show signs that it's maxed out. Entrepreneur Jon Miller pointed this out to me when we were talking about his time at Marketo: "When we hit that $20m–$30m revenue mark, we started seeing diminishing returns on inbound. I realized writing twice as many ebooks wasn't going to double pipeline. I needed a new engine for growth and to move up-market. This is when I started experimenting with outbound."

Mastering these four stages—Proof of Life, Optimize, Profit, and Double Down—gives you a structured way to ramp new channels without blowing your budget or wasting time. If a channel can't make it through these stages, it's time to cut your losses and move on.

One final note on channels. Testing is great, but once you find something that's working, it's time to focus on that channel. One mistake I made in the midgame of Carb.io was letting myself get distracted with too many experiments instead of continuing to focus on what was already working for us. I was so worried that the newsletter or SEO would suddenly stop producing that I was constantly searching for new channels. This diverted resources away from the channel that was bringing in most of our revenue.

But there's more to sustainable growth than finding a killer channel. As we ramped up our GTM, a few product issues were quietly building—problems we hadn't noticed in our rush to scale that would become glaring. We'll dive into those pitfalls in the next chapter.

## Doing the Math

A common mistake founders make when investing in GTM is not knowing what they're willing to invest to acquire a customer before they start spending. They skip over one of the most critical steps: the sales math. Without doing the math up front, you're flying blind, and no amount of effort will fix a funnel that just doesn't add up.

Let me give you an example. In 2015 we worked with a fast-growing startup with a pretty slick product for designers. They started using our email platform and were getting great results—well above our benchmark rates for replies and meetings booked. They scaled up quickly, onboarding more employees, eager to keep the momentum going. But here's where it got tricky. They were generating around 30 meetings a month through our platform, but it wasn't translating into the revenue they needed to be profitable. Their product's annual recurring revenue was only $1,200. To cover the $2,000 they were spending on our platform every month, they needed to close at least two deals, and that's before even factoring in the cost of paying their account executives to close those deals. By the time you add in those salaries and follow-up costs, they'd need to close four to six deals a month just to break even. The math just didn't work. They scaled up too quickly without calculating the real cost per deal.

If you're going to invest in a GTM channel, you need to do the math up front and figure out if it can actually get you where you need to go. It's not enough to hit benchmarks for meetings or reply rates. You have to consider the entire funnel—what percentage of those meetings will convert, what it costs to service each deal, and how much you need to make back to justify the spend. You also need to consider your total addressable market and what percentage of that market is reachable through the channel.

A final factor is your financing strategy. Are you venture-backed and chasing aggressive growth targets, like the T2D3 model?[36] Or are you bootstrapped and focused on growing profitably from day one? Somewhere in the middle? These

---

36 The T2D3 ("triple, triple, double, double, double") model is a growth framework for SaaS companies aiming to scale to a billion-dollar valuation. It means tripling annual recurring revenue two years in a row, then doubling it for three years (e.g., from $1m to $3m to $9m, then to $18m, $36m, and $72m). This road map helps entrepreneurs focus on aggressive yet structured expansion to hit major revenue milestones. For more information see Neeraj Agrawal, "Helping Entrepreneurs 'Triple, Triple, Double, Double, Double' to a Billion-Dollar Company," Battery, March 21, 2015, battery.com/blog/helping-entrepreneurs-triple-triple-double-double-double-to-a-billion-dollar-company.

decisions shape everything from how quickly you ramp to how you allocate resources. So before you move forward with any investments, pull out a spreadsheet, document your assumptions, and allocate a budget for each of your experiments. Forcing yourself to write them down and share them with the team can do wonders for helping keep everyone accountable.

**Bonus: Sales Development Math Resource**
Accompanying this book is a copy of a model that I built to help founders I work with understand the profitability of a sales development team. It looks at the cost of the program, revenue produced, and payback timing. Go to terrifyingart.com/resources to grab your free copy.

## The Channel Adoption Life Cycle

As someone who ran an outsourced sales development service for 12 years (shortly I'll explain why outsourcing is usually a terrible idea and I'm an idiot) I've seen just about every permutation of claims that outbound, cold calling, and cold email are dead. Anyone that says any channel 100 percent doesn't work is wrong. They might be directionally correct, but channels are rarely 100 percent dead. Channel effectiveness tends to decrease over time, but it can ebb and flow if you give it long enough. I wholeheartedly believe (or hope, at least) that there must be at least one person out there who's figured out how to book meetings using messenger pigeons.

A marketer I met once described this trend as channel arbitrage, where the people early to a new channel reap the greatest returns. Once everyone catches on, the channel becomes more crowded, conversion rates decrease, and costs rise. When I first started in sales development I only found two places to learn about cold email: my future cofounder Aaron Ross's book *Predictable Revenue*, and Bryan Kreuzberger's email list.[37] The information was scarce and sales leaders with cold email experience were even scarcer. Fast forward to today and most companies know what it is and how to do it. You can't go on LinkedIn without seeing someone saying Cold Email Is Dead, Long Live Cold Email. The easy wins with outbound are gone and getting an ROI requires building a complex set of team, process, and tooling.

The maturation process follows the Technology Adoption Life Cycle, popularized by management consultant Geoffrey Moore, in the way that the early adopters of a technology get most of the benefits and the late-arriving majority and laggards get the least. I've noticed that any demand-generation tactic or channel that we've used has followed a similar curve. A key difference is that as the channel becomes broadly adopted and conversion rates fall, early adopters react by improving their process, which increases the table stakes to be successful and drives up the cost to acquire a customer using that channel. I was building tools for sales development when this happened and we always compared it to the Cold War: It was an arms race, and whoever had the best access to information, technology, and process got the best results. Maybe we should have been thinking of it as a Channel Adoption Life Cycle.

Take cold email for example. In 2012, I could send a mail merge from Google Sheets and expect to see a reply rate of 10 percent to 20 percent. The biggest tool that existed at that stage was Yesware, but I don't recall them offering mail merges at the time. The information available about the channel was

---

37 Bryan is the founder of Breakthrough Email, a successful cold emailing system.

fairly low—Aaron Ross and Bryan Kreuzberger were the only people I found who were actually sharing information on how to do it. Many companies had heard about the channel but weren't sure how to implement it and scale it up. Some companies were resistant to the idea at a philosophical level, some people told me it would never work, some were upset we would consider something so unseemly, and most information technology folks were flat out against any cold email. Despite all this resistance, the conversion rates were fantastic. Most customers were booking 20 to 30 meetings a month off very basic lists.

### Channel Adoption Life Cycle

| | Information Availability | Tool Availability | Resistance to Implementation | Conversion Rate |
|---|---|---|---|---|
| **Innovators** | Very low | Very low | Very high | Extremely high |
| **Early Adopters** | Low | Low | High | Very high |
| **Early Majority** | Medium | Medium | Medium | High |
| **Late Majority** | High | High | Low | Medium |
| **Laggards** | Very high | Very high | Low | Low |

Using this example, the four characteristics of a channel adoption stage would be information availability, tool availability, resistance to implementation, and conversion rate.

The next time you're thinking about adopting a channel, take a moment to consider where it is in its life cycle adoption curve. Starting a new channel in either the earlier or the later stages will still be challenging, but for very different reasons.

## Why Outsourcing Sucks

Let me be clear: Outsourcing can work, but for most companies it's a recipe for wasted time and money. After 12 years of running an outsourcing agency, I've come to realize that while there's a narrow niche where outsourcing makes sense, for most growing companies it's a bad bet. Companies want to test the waters, spend a few months outsourcing, and expect results that justify the investment. Spoiler: That almost never happens, especially within the six months that most customers are willing to commit to. I'm not just talking about my 12 years running the outsourcing side of Predictable Revenue; I also run a quarterly meetup with fellow sales development agency owners and they have a similar sentiment.

The problem is that companies treat outsourcing like a magic bullet, expecting an external team to deliver results without putting in the necessary groundwork. I hear the same story over and over: "Let's give this a shot for three to six months and see if it works." Here's the hard truth—three to six months isn't nearly enough time to see meaningful results. It's common for companies to spend thousands on outsourcing, hit the six-month mark without getting ROI, and walk away frustrated. They're eager to test, quick to abandon, and disappointed when the results don't come fast enough. But the truth is, outsourcing for a few months never works, except to waste money and cause regret.

Building a sales development team, whether in-house or outsourced, takes time—12 months to establish and another

12 months to become ROI-positive. But when it's fully ramped, it can be one of your most profitable growth channels. If you outsource for just six months—the hardest, least profitable phase—and then evaluate the channel based on those numbers, you're making decisions with the worst possible data. It's no wonder outsourcing often feels like a failure; the math was never in your favor to begin with.

It gets worse when companies treat outsourcing as an A/B test: "Let's see if the outsourced team can outperform our internal team." It's never that simple. There are hundreds of variables in play and no outsourcing engagement can replicate the level of care, attention, and integration you get from an internal team. No outsourced team member will care as much as someone on your internal team. It's not that they don't want you to succeed, but there's a difference between being part of my company and part of yours. They're not living and breathing your product. And in outbound sales, where quality outreach makes all the difference, that disconnect is critical.

So why do companies keep falling for the outsourcing myth? Impatience. Outbound takes time to build. You're reaching out to people who don't know you and aren't actively looking to buy, and nurturing them into opportunities takes time. But most companies don't want to wait 12 months for results. They want leads now. So they think, "Let's just pay experts to do the heavy lifting." It's the classic shortcut mentality. Companies hit the six-month mark, see little return, and pull the plug—just as the seeds are starting to sprout.

Outsourcing only works under specific circumstances—and even then, it's the exception, not the rule. For it to succeed, you need three things:

**A well-defined market.** Outsourcing works best when you know exactly who your ideal customer is and your market is large enough to support an outbound strategy. Clear targeting reduces wasted time on bad leads and improves results. This needs to be communicated ahead of time and not be subject to constant change throughout the engagement.

**An integrated team.** You have to treat outsourced SDRs like internal hires. That means proper onboarding, training, and support. An SDR can only succeed if they understand your product, your market, and your buyer personas. Most outsourced SDRs fail because companies throw them a script and expect miracles.

**Time.** Outbound is a long game. Whether internal or external, SDRs need time to refine their approach, build relationships, and nurture leads. If you don't give an outsourced team the runway to deliver, you're setting them up to fail. I'm not saying you need to give them unlimited runway (especially if they're one of my competitors!), but don't expect miracles in the first six months.

Even with these elements in place, outsourcing is still a gamble. If you want to win at outbound, build your team in-house. Yes it's harder and takes more time, but the results are so much better. When you hire internally, you control everything—training, process, execution. Your team is an extension of your company's values, mission, and goals. They're personally invested in your success, and that translates into better results.

In addition, internal SDRs know the nuances of your market, adapt based on real feedback, and improve over time. While it might take longer to get your internal team ramped, they'll outperform any outsourced team in the long run. They're not working off a generic playbook—they're evolving alongside your company.

Outsourcing is not the magic bullet people want it to be. Instead, focus on building your own team, investing in their success, and playing the long game. Because in outbound sales, the long game is the only game worth playing.

One more note: After having this conversation with founders too many times, we decided to shut down our company's outsourcing line of business. We're now focused on helping founders find their first customers, build their first sales teams, and work go-to-market magic with tools like Clay.com.

## Founder-Led Prospecting

Below is the process I use whenever I'm launching (or advising on) a new startup's customer acquisition strategy. While some of these points might sound straightforward, executing them diligently—*by hand*, at first—makes all the difference.

**Pinpoint the Problem and Persona**

Before you do anything else, be absolutely clear on *what problem* you're solving and *who* you're solving it for. (If you haven't already, revisit "The MarketFit Process" section in chapter 4.) Identify the roles, industries, and specific titles of people who typically experience the pain your product addresses. This clarity keeps your prospecting tight and focused—no wasted outreach on people who don't need or appreciate what you're offering.

**Build a Target List**

Once you know who you want to reach, *start small*. I like to assemble an initial list of 50 to 100 prospects, maximum. That's enough for meaningful feedback but not so large that you lose the ability to verify each name. Why go small at first? By manually reviewing each contact—checking job titles, company type, and relevant pain points—you quickly see if your targeting is on track. This tight feedback loop prevents you from blasting the wrong message to a huge and inaccurate list. And when you create your list, make sure to document the context behind it. I recommend using our MarketFit Matrix—you can get a copy of the template at terrifyingart.com/resources.

**Get the Word Out**
When you're confident in your initial target list, it's time to craft your outreach—but keep it simple. I recommend starting with two channels:

**Cold email:** Aim for batches of about 30 prospects per day. You can send them manually or use a mail merge tool like Yet Another Mail Merge. At this volume, it's generally safe to use your main email account. Once you start sending more than 30 a day, you'll want to look into best practices for email deliverability to keep your domain reputation healthy. Note: At this stage I'm not sending follow-ups. If you plan on sending them, make sure your total email volume stays under 30 a day.

**LinkedIn:** Instead of sending an empty connection request, include your message in the connection note. This helps the prospect see immediately why you're reaching out and can encourage a faster response.

In both cases, avoid pitching. Lead with your focus and ask for advice. Keep it short, clear, and focused on starting a conversation—not closing a deal. By sending a small batch each day, you can quickly see how prospects respond and tweak your approach if you're not getting the replies you hoped for.

**Keep It Manual at First**
I recommend doing most of this process by hand initially, without relying on automation. That means no big mail merges or automated sequences just yet. Why? When you're typing or tailoring each message, you see firsthand which parts are clunky, which references might be wrong, and whether your targeting is

off. If you automate too early, you risk giving hundreds of prospects a message that's slightly off-target—and that leads to low response rates and misleading data.

**Track Every Response**
Finally, keep tabs on everything in a spreadsheet or lightweight CRM. Each prospect should have a status: Contacted, Replied, No Response, Not Interested, Booked a Call, etc. This lets you see patterns—do half the people open but never reply? Are people more likely to reply to one pain point than another one? Are they replying with a similar objection or not replying at all? Every data point you collect here is *pure gold* for refining your next batch of outreach.

That's the core of founder-led prospecting: a small, precise list, a clear hypothesis about who needs your solution, a tight feedback loop, and lots of manual work at first to confirm everything's on the right track. By the time you consider any form of automation—or bringing in a dedicated salesperson—you'll know exactly where the strongest signals are coming from and *why* your messaging resonates.

# EIGHT

# FOUR FUNNELS THAT DRIVE GROWTH

**A chain is only as strong as its weakest link.**

THOMAS REID[38]

**THE FIRST THING** to start eroding revenue at Carb.io wasn't a sales problem, it was a churn problem. Customers just weren't staying long enough to enable us to grow. New customers were still rolling in at a pretty good pace, but that was nullified because old customers were leaving at roughly the same rate. The result was the growth plateau I've shown you. We could have tried to push past it by dumping more money into customer acquisition, but that would have just accelerated our eventual demise. When I think back on our Growth Formula at that time, it's clear that our product-market fit had weakened. It was clearly a retention problem, but it was ultimately caused by a product issue, not a people issue.

However, while Carb.io was dying, our agency—Predictable Revenue—was growing, and we finally managed to catch up with our inbound leads enough to start building our own outbound team. Our first few months with outbound followed a familiar pattern: a bunch of meetings that went nowhere. This is pretty normal for a first attempt, and it's a reason why many people have had a bad experience with outbound. As we refined our targeting and messaging, though, we started having more

---

38  This expression first appeared in Thomas Reid's *Essays on the Intellectual Powers of Man* (John Bell/G.G.J. & J. Robinson, 1785).

sales conversations and prospects started entering the pipeline. Around the six-month mark we closed our first deal from outbound and we all celebrated, thinking the journey was over and it would be a *predictable revenue* source (get it?) for us moving forward. Then month 7 rolled around and outbound produced nothing.

Month 8 we closed a deal. Month 9 we didn't. No matter how we tweaked the targeting or messaging, this alternating pattern continued. It was just after the 12-month mark that we started seeing a deal close every month. We sat down with the team to figure it out, and our SDR, Peter Nieuwenburg, mentioned that during the first year he noticed that most of the people he talked to were the right folks, but outbound wasn't top of mind for them. So every time someone said they weren't ready, he made a point of adding them into a "nurture sequence" in his CRM so that he remembered to stay in touch.

When we looked at Peter's nurture sequences, we noticed a relatively low number of prospects and extremely high conversion rates. He had been working his nurture sequences every month or two and this was the source of additional deals. Most people he met through outbound weren't thinking about outbound when he met them. His creative persistence meant that his name was top of mind once they started to consider it. Most sales reps discard, ignore, or simply forget about the prospects that fall out of their pipeline because they're hard to keep track of. But Peter showed us the easy solution to this problem, and it dovetails nicely with the Next Action habit you learned in chapter 6.

Growth requires consistently engaging in four different functions: starting conversations with potential customers, turning those conversations into revenue, converting revenue into happy customers, and staying in touch with people who aren't ready to buy yet. These four functions form a chain-link system, meaning the strength of the whole is limited by the strength of the weakest link. I think of them as a simple multiplication equation where the result is the level of growth achieved. If I'm getting full marks for three of them but a zero for the other one, my total growth will be zero. It is the output of these numbers that feed the revenue execution number in the Growth Formula. Creating a repeatable revenue engine requires balancing these four functions. This chapter will help you understand what they are and how to build that engine yourself.

## Specialize Your Sales Functions

Take a look at your current pipeline. How many of the above functions are represented? Most pipelines I look at have at least a few different sales functions represented.

When I only had one, my biggest struggle was following up with opportunities that weren't going to move forward in the following 90 days. I had two options: leave them in my main funnel to sit there or mark them as Closed-Lost and set a reminder task to follow up on them. The problem with reminders is that they're low importance and low urgency and often pop up when I'm logging into the CRM to do something important, so they get ignored. Knowing this, I would let deals sit in my pipeline so long that it became clogged with dead opportunities that I had wanted to follow up on eventually.

Mixing dead deals with my live deals not only messed up all my conversion and timing metrics but also made my pipeline hard to read. Something I learned building voltageCRM was that a user can only process so much information on each page before they overload. The more data you put on the page, the more of their mental RAM you consume. So a user can either understand one thing on the page very deeply or process multiple things at a very shallow level. The same principle holds with our pipeline: The more deals that are in each stage, the less attention we can give to them.

I finally got fed up with my lack of follow-up and deleted Closed-Lost, replacing it with two labels: Closed-Lost-Not-ICP and Closed-Lost-Nurture. In Salesforce, I duplicated my current opportunity view and changed the filter to only show me deals labeled Closed-Lost-Nurture, and my nurture pipeline was born. I committed to reviewing next steps on my nurture opps every Friday afternoon and actioning 10 every time I do. This made it easier to actually follow up because I had a dedicated place to look, a committed time in my calendar to action the steps, and a quota for myself to hit. Follow-up went from something I might do to something that I consistently did a little of every week.

The greatest benefit to separating my deals this way went beyond simplifying my nurture process. It was the clarity that I now had in my main closing pipeline. Removing 100 stagnant opportunities allowed me to focus on the 30 I was actively trying to move forward. Removing surplus nurtures also enabled me to simplify my pipeline stages so that I could just focus on productive outcomes. It also brought back the velocity to my closing funnel. Now that deals weren't sitting in that funnel for months while I nurtured them, I could now measure how many deals I was actively working as opposed to nurturing. The difference might seem slight but the clarity I had every time I looked at my new pipeline was tremendous—Marie Kondo would have been proud. By splitting the two, it brought down my average time to close because now I was only measuring the length of time the deal was in my active pipeline. If I pushed it to nurture, the clock would run on my nurture timer instead of my closing timer.

Take a look at your current pipeline. How many of the processes I've described are represented by your pipeline stages?

If multiple funnels are lumped together, it's time for a change—specifically, time to specialize. Splitting your funnels this way offers clear benefits:

- **Fewer opps per pipeline:** You can more easily see where each account stands.

- **More relevant stages:** You'll define pipeline stages that actually match the steps needed to move an opportunity forward.

- **Clearer sales cycle data:** You'll see genuine movement between funnels, revealing the true length of your active sales process. Many companies assume their cycle is longer simply because they're mixing multiple funnels into one pipeline.

Here are your new funnels and their purpose:

- **Meet:** starting conversations with people outside your network

- **Discovery:** turning initial conversations into customers and revenue

- **Manage:** sustaining a base of happy long-term customers

- **Nurture:** maintaining relationships with prospects who are not ready to buy yet

## The Meet Funnel

The Meet Funnel is the entry point for starting conversations with potential customers. Its primary goal is to start conversations with people who could buy your product, feeding the rest of the sales process. Whether you're using outbound, inbound, paid ads, or partnerships, the Meet Funnel's purpose remains the same: to initiate contact with the right people and create a steady flow of opportunities.

A successful Meet Funnel is targeted, consistent, and can utilize multiple channels. It focuses on reaching accounts and personas that align with your Ideal Customer Profile (ICP). Consistency is critical—peaks and valleys in the frequency of meetings create instability throughout the sales process. Execution varies by channel: Outbound may involve personalized outreach, while inbound relies on optimized content and campaigns. Paid ads focus on ROI-driven lead generation, and partnerships expand reach through external networks. Regardless of the approach, the Meet Funnel must align with your product's price point, complexity, and market size.

The Meet Funnel directly impacts the success of the downstream funnels—Discovery (Disco), Manage, and Nurture. A weak Meet Funnel disrupts the entire sales system. High-quality leads that match your ICP are essential to ensure productive discovery calls in the Disco Funnel, while leads that aren't ready to engage should seamlessly transition to the Nurture Funnel instead of being discarded.

Common pitfalls in the Meet Funnel include generating low-quality leads due to poor targeting, failing to iterate and refine messaging or tactics, and prioritizing meeting volume over quality. These issues lead to inefficiencies and lower conversion rates in the later stages of the sales process. And one of the biggest mistakes I see founders make is doing a lot of customer development research when they're building their product, and then completely forgetting about it when they turn their attention to their revenue motion.

To avoid these problems, you need to make strategic decisions about channel fit, data quality, and the balance between efficiency and effectiveness. For example, low-cost products may benefit from a high-volume, low-touch strategy, while high-cost products require a personalized, high-touch approach.

Evaluating the Meet Funnel requires a focus on key metrics such as the number of meetings generated, lead quality, and rates of conversion to opportunities in the Disco Funnel. Iterative improvements are essential—regularly refining targeting, messaging, and tactics ensures the funnel remains effective over time. The Meet Funnel is not about quick wins but about building a reliable and consistent pipeline. Its success depends on discipline, alignment with the rest of the sales system, and a commitment to long-term growth.

By viewing the Meet Funnel as a dynamic and adaptable system, businesses can create a steady flow of high-quality opportunities that support sustainable growth across all of the sales process.

## Disco

The purpose of the Disco Funnel (short for Discovery) is to deeply understand the buyer's needs, assess alignment with your solution, and help them make a buying decision. It's where the interest generated in the Meet and Nurture Funnels gets converted into new customers and revenue.

A successful Disco Funnel prioritizes empathy, curiosity, and clarity over hard selling. The focus isn't on convincing a prospect to buy but on understanding their challenges, goals, and decision-making processes. Great discovery requires asking the right questions, listening carefully, and demonstrating expertise in your problem space. Reps who excel in the Disco Funnel don't push solutions—they guide buyers through the process, helping them uncover whether your product is the right fit.

One of the keys to an effective Disco Funnel is clear and objective pipeline stages. Each stage should have shared, verifiable definitions that leave no ambiguity about where a deal stands.

As an example, here are the stage definitions Jaimie Buss taught me in our podcast about how in 2018 she was forecasting $500m in revenue for Zendesk with 99 percent accuracy:

- **Stage 0**: Meeting booked—a meeting is scheduled with a prospective client.

- **Stage 1**: Qualify—the prospect attends the qualification call and agrees to a discovery call.

- **Stage 2**: Discovery—the prospect attends the discovery call and agrees to a demo with all relevant stakeholders.

- **Stage 3**: Solution review—the prospect confirms that "do nothing" is off the table and tech requirements have been met.

- **Stage 4**: Solution validation—prospect confirms that we are the consensus pick among stakeholders and shares their paperwork/legal process.

- **Stage 5**: Contracting/Verbal—economic decision-maker confirms decision and signs a contract.

- **Stage 6**: Closed-Won—a purchase order is issued or cash is in the bank (depending on the size of the deal).

- **Stage 7**: Closed-Nurture—the prospect is not ready to buy, so move them to the Nurture Funnel (I added this one).

These shared definitions ensure that every deal in the Disco Funnel is evaluated consistently across the team, improving forecasting accuracy and pipeline health.

Qualification frameworks like MEDDPICC or BANT[39] play a critical role in the Disco Funnel. These methodologies help teams measure the depth of understanding they have about each deal, such as the buyer's pain points, decision-making process, and economic motivations. A scoring system tied to these frameworks allows reps and managers to quickly assess the quality of an opportunity and identify gaps that need to be addressed. For example, scoring criteria like identified pain or decision criteria provide structure to what might otherwise be subjective judgments.

The Disco Funnel also thrives on simplicity and focus. A cluttered pipeline slows down a sales rep's decision-making and reduces velocity, so it's essential to keep the funnel clean by moving stalled deals to the Nurture Funnel or removing accounts that don't fit your ICP. With a focused Disco Funnel, teams can concentrate their efforts on active opportunities, leading to faster deal cycles and better close rates.

Ultimately, the Disco Funnel is about serving the buyer, not manipulating them. Success comes from helping prospects understand their challenges, guiding them through the decision-making process, and aligning your solution with their needs. When you build a Disco Funnel with clear processes, shared definitions, and a buyer-first mindset, you can turn interest into meaningful revenue while maintaining trust and credibility.

## Manage

The Manage Funnel is where revenue turns into long-term success. It focuses on delivering value to your customers, ensuring they achieve their desired outcomes, and creating opportunities for expansion through upselling or cross-selling. While the Disco Funnel gets deals across the finish line, the Manage

---

39  MEDDPICC stands for Metric, Economic Buyer, Decision Criteria, Decision Process, Paper Process, Identified Pain, Champion, and Competition. BANT stands for Budget, Authority, Need, Timing. See "The Value of Shared Definitions and Methodology" section later in this chapter for more details.

Funnel ensures those deals translate into happy, loyal customers who contribute to sustainable growth.

The Manage Funnel contains two revenue teams: customer success and account management. While these functions are often lumped together, they serve distinct purposes. Customer success focuses on helping customers realize the promised value of your product. It's about aligning their experience with the outcomes they expected when they signed the deal. Account management, on the other hand, focuses on identifying opportunities to expand your footprint within the account—whether that's selling additional products, increasing user counts, or moving them to a higher tier of service. Both are critical to the health of the Manage Funnel, but they require different approaches and skill sets.

A well-designed Manage Funnel starts with clear definitions and processes. First, you need to identify the key stages of customer engagement: onboarding, adoption, value realization, and expansion. Each stage should have clear criteria for progression, ensuring that your team knows exactly where a customer stands and what actions are required to move them forward. For example, onboarding might involve completing setup and training, while value realization focuses on measurable improvements for the customer using your product.

Clarity in the Manage Funnel not only drives customer satisfaction but also makes it easier to spot warning signs of churn. In his "The Science of Scaling" post, Mark Roberge notes that companies should optimize the path for customers to reach your leading indicators of customer retention—with Slack, this indicator was a company sending 2,000 messages in their first 30 days. This proactive approach ensures customers stay engaged and continue to see value, which is critical for retention.

The Manage Funnel also plays a key role in identifying expansion opportunities. Happy customers are more likely to invest further in your product, but they need to see consistent value before committing to upsells or cross-sells. Account managers must stay in close contact with customers, understanding their evolving needs and demonstrating how additional solutions can help them achieve even greater outcomes. Regular check-ins and value-driven conversations ensure that opportunities for expansion are identified and acted upon at the right time.

One of the most significant advantages of a strong Manage Funnel is the flywheel effect it creates. Retained customers not only contribute recurring revenue but also become advocates for your product, driving referrals and improving your reputation in the market. This effect accelerates growth by turning happy customers into a powerful demand generation channel.

The Manage Funnel is where revenue finds its second life. It's not just about keeping customers—it's about making them successful and helping them grow alongside your business. With a structured funnel, clear roles, and a focus on delivering consistent value, the Manage Funnel transforms customer relationships into a long-term growth engine.

## Nurture

The Nurture Funnel bridges the gap between initial engagement and future opportunities, ensuring that promising leads who aren't ready to buy today remain in your orbit until they are. It's where you build relationships with prospects who align with your ICP but aren't yet in a buying cycle. The Nurture Funnel prevents valuable leads from slipping through the cracks—it turns "not now" into "yes down the road."

A well-designed Nurture Funnel starts with clear criteria for what belongs in it. Leads should meet your ICP and show potential but lack the immediate need, budget, or timing to move forward. Instead of marking them as "lost," transition them into a nurture pipeline with a clear plan for staying engaged. This simple shift keeps your active pipelines clean while giving nurture leads the attention they deserve.

The key to the Nurture Funnel is consistency. Effective nurturing isn't about high-volume automation—it's about periodic, thoughtful follow-ups that maintain the relationship. Assign reps a regular cadence, such as reviewing and contacting a set number of nurture accounts weekly. These touchpoints can be as simple as sharing relevant content, checking in on progress, or providing insights that demonstrate your ongoing value.

One of the biggest advantages of a Nurture Funnel is clarity. By separating nurture leads from active opportunities, your main pipeline becomes easier to manage, and your team can focus on closing deals that are ready to move forward. Meanwhile, the Nurture Funnel creates a safe landing zone for long-term opportunities, reducing the risk of leads being forgotten or deprioritized.

For nurturing to succeed, there must be a system in place to prevent leads from going dormant. For example:

- Require reps to touch each nurture account quarterly.

- Use CRM views or automation to organize and surface nurture accounts.

- Set quotas for manual follow-ups to ensure consistent effort without overwhelming your team.

When done right, the Nurture Funnel resolves the tension between teams focusing on demand generation and closing. Demand teams can focus on bringing in high-quality leads, while closing teams maintain lean pipelines of active opportunities, knowing that nurture leads are being handled systematically. This shared understanding improves collaboration and pipeline health across the board.

The Nurture Funnel is the ultimate insurance policy for your sales process. By investing in long-term relationships, you build a pipeline of future opportunities while keeping your active pipeline clean and efficient. Over time, these efforts pay dividends as nurtured leads transition into ready-to-buy customers, often with higher conversion rates than cold outreach. The Nurture Funnel isn't just a backup plan—it's a critical part of a sustainable growth strategy.

A note on implementing the four funnels: Do not feel like you now need to have a specific pipeline in your CRM for each of these funnels. In our Salesforce, I have a Closed-Lost-Nurture status in my Disco pipeline and a custom view that only shows deals in that stage (along with next actions and next action dates). This is a good enough system for our small team and we have more complex automations running in our sales engagement tool, Apollo.io. Remember, the two most important pieces are a separate view (to reduce cognitive load) and the ability to measure the funnel metrics. You can check both of those boxes with a spreadsheet or a Notion table.

If you just opened your CRM to add all the funnels, close it. Seriously, the juice isn't worth the squeeze until you have more than a few sales reps. Don't spend good time on this when there are other high-priority jobs to be done.

## The Value of Shared Definitions and Methodology

Shared definitions are the foundation of pipeline clarity. Without clear, objective definitions and consistent qualification standards, pipelines become chaotic, making it nearly impossible to forecast accurately or identify real opportunities. These definitions ensure everyone on the team speaks the same language, evaluates deals consistently, and maintains a clean, actionable pipeline.

Shared definitions eliminate ambiguity in pipeline stages. When each stage has clear, verifiable criteria, there's no room for subjective interpretation. For example, a stage like Discovery might require that all decision-makers have attended a meeting, while Solution Review may require confirmation that your product meets the customer's technical requirements. These objective markers ensure that opportunities move through the pipeline based on progress, not gut feel.

Without shared definitions, pipelines become a mess. Reps may overestimate deal readiness, clogging the funnel with unqualified or stagnant opportunities. Managers can't trust the data, making it difficult to coach effectively or forecast accurately. Shared definitions create order from chaos, ensuring every deal in the pipeline reflects reality.

A qualification methodology provides a structured way to assess the health of each deal. Frameworks like MEDDPICC or BANT help teams consistently evaluate key criteria, such as the buyer's pain points and decision-making process, and the potential value of the solution. By scoring deals against these criteria, you gain a clear picture of which opportunities are worth pursuing and where gaps need to be addressed.

For example, MEDDPICC evaluates all areas of a deal—such as metrics, economic buyer, identified pain, and decision process—and gives them a score of either 0 (no information has been gathered), 1 (partial knowledge), or 2 (complete understanding, with actionable insights).

This scoring system allows reps and managers to objectively assess how well an opportunity is progressing and identify areas for improvement. Over time, the methodology becomes a shared playbook for evaluation, reducing variability across the team.

Combining shared definitions with a qualification methodology creates a pipeline that is not only clean but actionable:

- **Clarity across the team:** Every rep evaluates opportunities using the same standards, making it easy to compare pipelines and coach effectively.
- **Improved forecasting:** With objective criteria and consistent qualification, managers can confidently predict outcomes and identify risks.
- **Better coaching:** Managers can pinpoint where deals are getting stuck and coach reps on specific gaps, such as identifying the economic buyer or quantifying pain.

To implement this system effectively:

- **Document your definitions:** Clearly define each pipeline stage with objective, externally verifiable criteria.
- **Adopt a qualification methodology:** Choose a framework like MEDDPICC or BANT, and train your team to apply it consistently.
- **Score deals regularly:** Use a scoring system to evaluate deals based on qualification criteria and track progress over time.
- **Enforce consistency:** Regularly review pipelines to ensure reps are following the framework, and randomly test reps to confirm understanding.

Pipeline clarity isn't just about cleaning up your CRM—it's about creating a system that everyone can trust. With shared definitions and a qualification methodology in place, your pipeline becomes a true reflection of your sales process, enabling better decisions and driving consistent growth.

## Don't Buy a CRM

I bet all this talk about shared definitions got you charged up to go out and invest in a new CRM tool or maybe even clean up the one you're currently not using. Here's a better idea: Don't do it. (As noted in chapter 6, I have a free spreadsheet you can use instead. It's available at terrifyingart.com/resources.)

I'll add a little more context. Many founders in my network know me as the dummy who started a CRM company, so they come to me when they are getting ready to start selling and want to buy sales software. The short answer is that they don't need a CRM, they need a place to keep track of the deals they're working, and at this stage a spreadsheet is going to be the best tool for the job.

You may be thinking, "But mine connects to my email" or "It syncs with my marketing stack." Who cares? It only matters if you're going to use it and use it enough to justify the investment of money and, more importantly, your time researching, buying, and setting it up. Here's the biggest reason you don't need a CRM: Most founders I've talked to have spent more time researching and setting up their CRM than actually using it. It doesn't mean CRM is bad, it's just not something you need right now.

Another problem with CRM is that most founders don't set it up correctly in the first place. Even if they do use it, they're not going to use it right. No judgment if you've just bought a CRM, a contacts database, or a sales engagement tool. I've been there too. When you're a founder doing something new, there is so much uncertainty that buying and setting up a new tool feels like making progress. But it can be a time hole of dopamine hits that doesn't help you move the company forward. It's not just CRM—I once spent a month working with a mentor on a delivery schedule spreadsheet for our consulting team and it was beautiful, functional, and accomplished everything they could possibly want. The problem? Just doing things in their email was easier, so our perfect sheet was never used.

As founders, time is our most scarce resource, so we need to find the minimum effective dose instead of the absolutely perfect solution. My spreadsheet has 80 percent of the functionality—that people actually use—of Salesforce, it can be implemented very quickly, and it's 100 percent free.

OK, it's not free. It'll cost you time to figure out how to use it, time to decide whether to move from your current system to this sheet, and an increase in the risk of forgetting a deal when you switch from one tool to another.

So let me walk you through the key points of the sheet. As discussed in chapter 6, the key fields are: Deal Name, Contact Name, Opportunity Stage, Next Action, Next Action Date, and Notes. Those are the basics and tell you where you are in your process and what you need to do next. Here's what you need to know:

- The Opportunity Stage tells you what has happened so far.
- Next Action is what you need to do next to move the deal forward.
- Next Action Date is when that action will happen.

I'm a big fan of David Allen and his book *Getting Things Done* and 100 percent stole this idea from him. (For a great one-minute explainer, go to next.terrifyingart.com to see a video called "Can you explain the process of dealing with 'next actions'? by David Allen" on the Russell Sarder channel.) The core idea is that at the end of every meeting with a prospect, you decide on what to do next, write it down, and pick a date it needs to happen on. This frees your mind because you can forget about the deal until that time makes its way to the top of your list. It's even more powerful if you and the prospect agree on what to do next while you're still on the call and book it into your calendar. This is especially efficient because it saves you all the headache of following up and getting something scheduled. If the prospect is going to move forward, you may as well get it booked now and save everyone the hassle.

As I emphasized earlier, your sales stages should be mapped to objective outcomes. I've put Disco Funnel stages into the spreadsheet template; I stole them from Jaimie Buss when she was VP of sales for Zendesk and forecasting revenue with 99 percent accuracy.[40] These are also the stage definitions we've been using internally at Predictable Revenue since I interviewed Jaimie. Jaimie's process was slightly heavier than what we needed because they were selling larger and more complex deals, so here are the stages we use internally today (note that all these stages are verified by customer actions):

1. **Qualify:** Customer attends call and agrees to the next one.

2. **Discovery:** They attend call and agree to bring any key stakeholders to the next one.

3. **Solution Review:** They confirm that "do nothing" is off the table. This means they've decided to make a change but haven't decided on using us yet.

4. **Solution Validation:** They confirm our solution will meet their need, confirm the paper process, and confirm that all stakeholders are aligned.

5. **Contracting/Verbal:** Economic buyer confirms decision, signs contracts/documents.

6. **Closed-Won:** Customer pays.

---

[40] Find out more by watching our podcast conversation or reading the related blog post, both of which are available at zendesk.terrifyingart.com.

7  **Closed-Lost-Nurture:** Customer is not ready to make a change.

8  **Closed-Lost-Competitor:** They went with a competitor.

9  **Closed-Lost-FOAD:** They told us to leave them alone and perish.[41]

You'll notice that these are just the stages for the Disco Funnel. The Nurture Funnel doesn't need complicated stages as long as you're updating and working your next actions regularly. The stages in your Manage Funnel will vary based on the steps required to onboard new customers and make them successful. For the Meet Funnel I've gone with the following stages:

0  **Cold:** The prospect has been added to a list.

1  **Approaching:** We have begun reaching out over any channel.

2  **Connected:** The prospect replied or answered a call and didn't tell us to leave them alone and perish (FOAD).

3  **Meeting Booked:** They have agreed to attend a discovery meeting.

4  **Meeting Held:** They showed up to the discovery meeting.

5  **Moved to Disco:** They agreed to a second call and have been moved to the Disco Funnel.

6  **FOAD:** They asked us to leave them alone and perish.

Now that you have the definitions, the next step is to figure out how much you know about each deal. That's where a qualification methodology comes in. You can use MEDDPICC, BANT,

---

41  You might notice that the acronym doesn't quite line up. It's crude, so we opted to leave it out, but I bet you could guess it pretty easily. Shout-out to Carrie Simpson, who originally introduced me to the acronym.

or any other framework, as long as you use it consistently. The information you get from it is a good proxy for how much you can trust the sales stage. A good MEDDPICC score of 14/16 does not indicate that the deal is 88 percent likely to close—it tells us we know 88 percent of the information that we'd like to about this opportunity. I've included columns for MEDDPICC in the spreadsheet because that's what I like to use, but it doesn't matter if you use a different framework. There are two columns for each framework criterion, a score and a note field. The scoring system is: 0 = "I know nothing," 1 = "I know something," and 2 = "I know everything I need to." The note field is for you to back up your score so someone like me can test if you really have a 2/2 for your economic buyer. Here are the framework criteria:

> *Metric:* How you quantify the potential gain from the identified pain
> 
> *Economic Buyer:* The person who will write the check
> 
> *Decision Criteria:* The criteria for technical and business requirements
> 
> *Decision Process:* The process followed by stakeholders, influencers, and approvers to determine whether to buy
> 
> *Paper Process:* The process required to make the purchase
> 
> *Identified Pain:* The specific challenge(s) at the company that your product would solve
> 
> *Champion:* The person who has the power, influence, and something to gain by adopting your solution
> 
> *Competition:* Who are you up against? Another company or "do nothing"?

Your pipeline stage, next actions, and qualification methodology are the holy trinity of a great sales process. They tell you where you are, what happens next, and how much you can trust your information. When you use them consistently, they also can tell you where your gaps are and what to do to fill them. If you nail those three things, you'll be in a better spot than 80 percent of sales organizations.

When do you *need* to buy a CRM? You'll feel it. But here are some things to watch out for: You have multiple salespeople in a spreadsheet at once, your browser slows down when you open it, and a deal got forgotten about because there's too much happening. I've seen companies with big sales teams run on sheets, and most big companies that use CRMs export a bunch of their data to sheets anyway. So why not just skip the middleman and stay in sheets? At least for a while.

Go to terrifyingart.com/resources for your copy of the sheet. For a look at the CRM alternative, you can also find a screenshot of what our Salesforce looks like with the four funnels added in. If you're dead set on buying a CRM, check out Clarify (getclarify.ai).

# HIRE AND MANAGE YOUR FIRST SALESPERSON

Taking on a challenge is a lot like riding a horse.
If you're comfortable while you're doing it,
you're probably doing it wrong.

TED LASSO[42]

**C**ONGRATULATIONS! You've found product-market fit, you've built a system for consistent revenue, and you probably have that $1 million in annual income in your sights. But now you're so busy running the company that you just don't have the bandwidth to keep doing all the selling yourself. You've been an incredible salesperson—nobody knows the product like you do—but it's time to hand off the day-to-day sales tasks and get back to working *on* the business, not *in* it. If you're here, congratulations, you did the hard part and survived. Now the really hard part starts. But you can do it.

How you pull yourself out will vary based on where your business is at. My first hire was an account executive because the top of our funnel was very strong (about 40–60 meetings a month) due to the well-timed acquisition of the Predictable Revenue brand. If I didn't have that luxury, I would have started by hiring a sales development rep to help me build pipeline so I could keep closing. I was having this conversation with a mentor of mine, Lars Nilsson, and he strongly recommended starting with a content marketing hire, then two business development reps, then an account executive, a revenue operations lead, and a customer success rep. (You can read more about Lars's approach at lars.terrifyingart.com.)

---

42  *Ted Lasso*, "Pilot," season 1, episode 1, November 12, 2019.

Think of this method of growing your early team as bottleneck scaling—pushing the boundaries of an individual role until the need for the new hire becomes undeniable. Think of a founder in a full-cycle sales role: In addition to their regular founder duties, they also need to prospect, close, and manage customers. Now imagine that founder is the only one on the org chart and they occupy all of the roles. When you run into a bottleneck you hire someone to fix it, thus building out the org chart from the founder down.

When you're building a new revenue team, there are going to be four major bottlenecks that you'll run into, and chances are you'll hit them in this order:

1. Content
2. Lead flow
3. Closing capacity
4. Management capacity

Your first revenue hire should be someone who can create content and build a digital presence. Lars points out that sales reps, including the founder, "can't do much if they can't educate or inspire," which requires content. This will look like case studies, copy for your website, and content for your blog and social media accounts. It needs to share your perspective on the problem space. The early goal for this hire is to arm the sales team with content and build a digital presence that prospective customers can trip over. I still remember the moment we published our first few case studies because the very next month our close rate went up 30 percent. They were such a powerful tool to show future customers they could trust us.

The next bottleneck is lead flow, and as Lars said, "The hardest part of closing any deal is finding it." If your content strategy is executed properly, if you're tapping into a HILS (high-importance, low-satisfaction) problem, and if people in your target market consume work-related web content, then you have a chance at generating some inbound leads. If you're in a space where inbound won't work, then you'll need to go outbound. I recommend doubling down on whatever is booking your meetings until you run into your next bottleneck, closing capacity.

The goal of an early sales development rep (SDR) and demand generation team is to fill up the calendar of the founder. Once the founder is so busy they can't run your business anymore, hire a full-cycle sales rep who's hungry and can step into a head-of-sales role after a year.

You may need to load-balance by alternating between hiring for lead flow or for closing capacity depending on where your bottleneck is. With two to five team members you're going to be pretty maxed for capacity and won't have the time to dedicate to properly managing all of them. Now is the time to promote an internal hire into a management role. In the early days, so much of your success will have come from your ability to learn what the market needs, and nobody will have been in a better position than one of your first account executives (AEs).

But before you can start hiring, you need to build the process that the new hires will be taught. That will be our focus for this chapter: getting you to document what you've learned and hire people to replace you. This process-building and hiring loop will enable you to slowly develop a sales organization underneath you that will enable you to get back to working on the business.

Hiring your first sales rep can feel like walking a tightrope without a net. You're stretched thin, juggling the demands of running the company while trying to keep your pipeline alive. Every deal feels crucial, and the idea of handing over such a critical piece of the business to someone else can feel both exciting and terrifying. What if they don't get it? What if they can't sell the way you can? What if they tank your early momentum?

I've been there. When we hired our first sales rep, I was extremely nervous to let go. Things were going well and I was terrified of screwing it up. Fortunately, I lucked out with our first rep, Kay—she came highly recommended by one of our coaches and turned out to be an absolute pro. But trying to find a second "Kay" proved far more challenging. We learned plenty of hard lessons along the way: what not to do, how to separate true talent from someone who just sounds good in an interview, and how much effort it takes to build a repeatable sales process. I learned these lessons the hard way—by screwing things up, pissing people off, and losing deals. Starting my career in sales helped, but being good at selling is a very different sport than building a revenue organization. You'll make mistakes too, and it'll be OK.

Maybe you're wrestling with similar challenges. You might be wondering if you've found the right hire, or you might be struggling to teach them how to replicate your success. Perhaps you've already brought someone on but their productivity has slowed, and you're stuck asking yourself, "Do I fire them? Do I give them another shot? Or is this all just part of the process?" Sound familiar? If not, welcome to the world of sales. It might feel chaotic and overwhelming right now, but there's a method to the madness—and we'll get through it together. Hiring and managing your first sales rep is less about hoping they'll figure it out and more about creating a foundation they can build on. There are three critical pillars to making this work, and they all boil down to one thing: process. Without it, you're leaving everything up to chance.

First, remember all the work you've already put into building a consistent, scalable sales approach in the last two chapters—that's the foundation your new hire will need. It's time to document what's made you successful so far. Founders have unique advantages: a deep understanding of the problem space, credibility from their title, and an innate ability to connect the product with customers. But those strengths don't automatically transfer to a sales rep. If you don't have a clear, repeatable process to hand off, you're setting them up to fail.

Second, you need a structured process for hiring. Great salespeople don't just walk in off the street—and even if they did, you'd need to know how to spot them. That's where a framework like the WHO method comes in. Originally laid out in *Who: The A Method for Hiring* by Geoff Smart and Randy Street, it provides a structured way to evaluate candidates based on their past performance, culture fit, and potential. We've tailored this approach specifically for hiring SDRs and AEs, helping us avoid costly mis-hires. I'll detail the high-level process and the adjustments we've made later in this chapter.

Finally, you need a process for managing reps once they're on board. Hiring is just the start—what you do afterward determines whether they'll succeed. This chapter will walk you through the three things you need to do every week to keep your team running smoothly: pipeline review, call review, and one-on-ones. These aren't just meetings; they're the backbone of how you'll develop and scale your sales team.

Mastering these three processes—documenting your success, hiring right, and managing effectively—will give you the tools to turn your first sales hire into a long-term win. Let's break them down.

## The Founder Advantage

As a founder, you bring unique strengths to the sales process—advantages that your first hire won't naturally possess. These strengths make you highly effective at selling your product but can also create blind spots when handing sales to someone else.

To set your sales rep up for success, you need to build processes and training that compensate for these blind spots.

First, you have an unmatched understanding of the problem space. You're the one who discovered the gap, spoke to potential customers, and developed the solution. That experience gives you a deep insight into your prospects' challenges, the solutions they've tried, and why those solutions fell short. You know how to empathize with your buyers, anticipate objections, and craft a pitch that resonates. Your new rep won't have that level of insight on day one. To bridge this gap, your process needs to help them learn the problem space quickly. Training materials, shadowing your calls, or having the rep interview customers themselves are great ways to build this foundational knowledge.

Second, there's the credibility boost of your title. As a founder or CEO, your words carry extra weight. Prospects are naturally more open to hearing your pitch because they know you've built the product and are deeply invested in its success. Your sales rep won't have that advantage and will need to rely on skill, persistence, and a well-built process to establish trust and authority. And recognize that what works for you might not work for them. Your sales system should reflect this and be designed to succeed without the "founder halo effect."

Finally, no one will ever match your passion for the product—it's your creation. While that level of emotional investment is hard to replicate, a great salesperson can become just as committed to the outcomes your product delivers. To help them get there, equip them with the tools, stories, and data they need to connect with prospects and clearly communicate your product's value.

When you document your process, think about how to translate your founder-level advantages into systems and training. How can you teach your understanding of the problem?

How do you compensate for the title boost your rep won't have? And how do you instill the confidence and product knowledge they'll need to succeed? Answering these questions will make your first hire more effective—and take your sales engine one step closer to scaling without you.

## Documenting the Process

If you've been running the sales process yourself, chances are you've relied on instinct—adjusting on the fly as situations arise. But your instincts aren't teachable, and when it's time to hire your first salesperson, relying on intuition alone won't cut it. To give your new rep the best chance of success, you need to transform your mental playbook into a documented process. Without this, your hire will flounder, and you'll spend more time fixing mistakes than you saved by hiring them.

Documenting your process is about consistency and scalability. It ensures that every prospect gets a consistent experience and that your sales outcomes aren't tied to one person's talent. As your team grows, having a solid playbook prevents chaos and helps you scale faster.

Start by defining the stages of your sales pipeline. For each stage, clearly outline the objective, criteria for progression, and examples of good execution. Identify your key buyer personas: what pain points they experience, what goals they're pursuing, and what objections they commonly raise. Capture your value proposition, clearly articulating how your product solves their problems and why it matters.

Next, write down the most common objections you face and how you handle them. Document how you run a demo highlighting key features and tying those features to value. Include your follow-up strategy—when to reach out, how often, and which messages have been most effective. Don't forget to list the tools you use, whether it's a CRM, email automation, or scheduling app. Even a simple resource guide will help your hire navigate the role more effectively.

This process doesn't have to be perfect at the start. Begin with a rough draft in Google Docs or Notion and focus on capturing what works. Iterate over time. Your new salesperson can provide feedback and help refine the system as they ramp up. This not only improves the process but also gives them a sense of ownership.

A documented sales process takes what you've learned and makes it repeatable. It bridges the gap between founder-led sales and a scalable system. Without it, you're gambling on your hire's ability to figure things out. With it, you're giving them—and your company—the tools to succeed. (I've put together a cheat sheet to help you with this. Grab your free copy at terrifyingart.com/resources.)

One more tip: Record your sales calls. If you're serious about building a scalable sales process, this is a must. It's a simple habit with big benefits. First, as I wrote in chapter 6, recording your calls makes it easier to review what's working (and what's not) in your approach. But second, it also provides invaluable content for onboarding new reps. Let them listen to how you handle objections, pitch your product, and navigate tough conversations. And finally, it sets a powerful precedent: Feedback is part of the company culture. When your team sees that even the founder is open to critique, it encourages them to embrace the same mindset.

So whether you're using a dedicated tool like Gong or Chorus, or just recording through Zoom, start building your library of calls. It's one of the most effective ways to turn your experience into a resource that helps your team grow.

## What to Expect When You're Hiring Your First Salesperson

Hiring the right salesperson isn't quick or easy. Finding a great candidate takes time and a structured process. You'll screen resumes, conduct interviews, and evaluate candidates through multiple stages. Even with an efficient process, this is a significant investment of your time and energy.

Expect to spend time clarifying what you need before the first interview happens. What kind of salesperson are you looking for? How much experience do they need? What goals do you have for them six months or a year down the road? Once you've defined the role, you'll move into the practical side of hiring—writing a job description, reviewing applications, conducting interviews, and checking references.

It's tempting to shortcut this process, especially when you feel you've found "the one." But skipping steps increases the risk of a bad hire—a mistake that can cost you months of lost time and productivity. Trust the process, and be prepared to meet many candidates before finding the right fit. Each interview will also help you refine what you're looking for, so the time spent is never wasted.

While hiring a salesperson has clear benefits, it's important to go in with open eyes about the trade-offs. Training a new hire is a time commitment, and their success depends on your willingness to invest in their development. At the same time, handing over sales means losing some of the direct customer insights you gain when you handle it yourself. This is why it's crucial to maintain open communication with your rep and create a system for gathering feedback from the field.

Hiring and onboarding your first salesperson might feel daunting, but it's a necessary step in building a scalable sales function. With the right mindset and a commitment to the process, you can set your new hire—and your business—up for long-term success.

## A Process for Hiring Salespeople

The two most important steps to hiring anyone are to have a process that everyone follows for *every* candidate and to use a scorecard for *every* interview. The combination of the two is what gives me confidence in my team's ability to hire. There are very few things that are unchangeable at Predictable Revenue, but our hiring process is at the top of that short list. People are our most important asset and we need a great process to consistently hire great people. Nearly every time I've skipped steps, I've regretted it.

When you get to the process, the first objection you're going to have is that it's too much work and it's too long—no great candidates are going to subject themselves to all of it. In my experience, it's been the opposite: Great candidates expect the process to be challenging. They respect it because it means you have set a high bar for hires, and great people want to work with other great people. Yes, you can find and hire talented people with a low-quality, quick and easy process, but it's *much* riskier and less consistent.

If you're new to hiring, I highly recommend picking up a copy of *Who: The A Method for Hiring*—its process is incredible for hiring senior talent. At Predictable Revenue, we've adapted the WHO method specifically for hiring SDRs and AEs. Our approach is structured around a series of interviews, each designed to evaluate key traits and skills systematically. The process begins with a screening interview, followed by a WHO interview, three focus interviews, and finally one for culture fit.

Throughout each stage, we rely on the STAR method (Situation, Task, Action, Result) to dig deeper into candidates' experiences and capabilities. This framework helps us explore not just what candidates claim to have done, but how they approached challenges and achieved results. For example, if a candidate mentions being creative, we might prompt them with, "Tell me about a time when you used your creativity in a work setting." From there, we use techniques like labeling ("That sounds intense"), paraphrasing, and pausing to encourage more detailed responses. This approach ensures we uncover meaningful insights while maintaining a conversational tone.

One thing we learned from books on the Entrepreneurial Operating System (EOS) was about scorecards. They've simplified their hiring scorecards into two sections, Values Alignment and Get It, Want It, and Have the Capacity. The best place to start with EOS is a book called *Traction* by Gino Wickman.[43] After each interview, everyone involved fills out a scorecard to grade each candidate on four key company-culture values, as well as each of these questions: Do they get it? Do they want it? Do they have the capacity?

### The Screening Interview

The screening interview is a quick, 30-minute session designed to assess whether the candidate has the basic skills and mindset required for the role. It's also an opportunity to identify any red flags or deal-breakers early on. We follow a consistent structure to ensure fairness and thoroughness.

---

43 Gino Wickman, *Traction: Get a Grip on Your Business* (BenBella Books, 2012). I've also adapted the EOS approach into my scorecard. Grab a copy of our internal scorecard at terrifyingart.com/resources, or eos.terrifyingart.com to get yours from EOS Worldwide.

We start by explaining that this is the first of five to seven interviews and that there are no trick questions—just a straightforward assessment. Questions include: "What are you really good at?" and "What are you not good at or not interested in doing?" The goal is to get candidates to share 7–10 examples for each. We also ask about their past managers, their career goals, and their salary expectations. For example, when asking about previous bosses, we say, "Who were your last five managers? What was it like working for them? And when we call them, what will they rate your performance on a scale of 1 to 10?" This makes it clear that reference checks are a standard part of the process.

**The WHO Interview**
This is the heart of our hiring process. It dives deep into the candidate's work history to uncover their real accomplishments. Using the WHO framework,[44] we ask the same five questions for each of their past roles: "What were you hired to do? What did you accomplish? What mistakes did you make? Who did you work with, and what would they say about you? Why did you leave?" This structured approach ensures we don't miss any critical details about their performance and capabilities.

By focusing on past behavior, we can identify patterns of success and failure, giving us a clear picture of how the candidate might perform in the role.

---

44 WHO stands for What you want (defined using a scorecard for the role's mission, outcomes, and required competencies), How you're going to get it (using a talent pipeline), and Objective evaluation of candidates (through structured interviews and reference checks).

### SDR Focus Interviews

The focus interviews for Sales Development Representatives are designed to assess their curiosity, grit, creativity, and ability to perform under pressure. Each interview targets specific traits to ensure we identify candidates who can handle the unique challenges of the role.

**Core values:** The first interview explores how well the candidate aligns with our company values. We ask them to share stories that demonstrate these values, such as, "Tell me about a time when your team had to take care of each other." Using techniques like labeling ("That sounds challenging") and paraphrasing ("So you handled that entirely on your own?"), we dig deeper into their answers. This helps us gauge whether they genuinely embody the principles our team lives by and how naturally they align with our culture.

**Performance:** The second interview tests the candidate's sales skills in a practical setting. If the candidate has prior sales experience, we ask them to pitch a product and handle objections. Halfway through, we provide feedback and challenge them to adjust their approach based on the coaching. The goal isn't perfection but to see how effectively they incorporate feedback into their process. For candidates without direct sales experience, we ask them to demonstrate something they're passionate about—a school project, a previous customer interaction, or even a hobby. This gives us insight into their confidence, adaptability, and ability to perform under pressure.

**Hustle, creativity, and fun:** The third interview delves into the candidate's work ethic, problem-solving abilities, and personality. Questions range from practical, like "What was the toughest job you've ever had?" to more creative prompts, such as "Can you write a haiku right now?" or "What random thing are you really awesome at?" These discussions help us assess the candidate's mindset, creativity, and how well they'll integrate into our team's culture.

### AE Focus Interviews

The focus interviews for account executives are structured to evaluate key skills and traits essential for navigating complex sales cycles, positioning against competition, and driving revenue. Each interview targets a critical dimension of success in the AE role.

**Sales philosophy:** The first interview examines the candidate's approach to sales and their ability to manage core responsibilities. We begin by discussing their past goals and metrics to understand how they measure success and whether they're results-driven. Even if the AE has worked with SDR support, we explore how they handle prospecting to ensure they can keep their pipeline full when needed.

Next, we evaluate their organizational skills by asking how they follow up on deals that haven't closed. This sheds light on their persistence and discipline. From there, we dive into their approach during sales calls: How do they connect product features to value? This question tests their ability to align solutions with buyer pain points. Finally, we ask them to walk us through their demo process, assessing their preparation, delivery, and ability to engage prospects effectively.

**Technical acumen and intellectual curiosity:** The second interview focuses on learning ability, adaptability, and technical comfort. We start by asking about the most recent thing they've learned, which showcases their curiosity and drive for self-improvement. We then dig into a challenging skill or task they've had to learn in a previous role, including what they struggled with and how they overcame it.

To test their technical competence, we ask about the most advanced thing they can do on a computer, ensuring they can work efficiently with modern tools. We round out the interview with questions about their reading habits, particularly sales-related books, to gauge their commitment to professional growth.

**Selling against the competition:** The final interview evaluates the candidate's ability to position effectively against competitors. We ask them to outline their competitors from a previous role and describe how they positioned themselves against each. This helps us understand their ability to identify strengths, weaknesses, and differentiation points.

We also dive into specific scenarios, such as handling tough competition or dealing with customer types that lean toward competitors. How did they position their solution? What strategies did they use to win the deal? These questions reveal how well the candidate understands market dynamics and adapts their approach to various sales situations.

**Why these questions matter:** Both the SDR and AE focus interviews aim to uncover critical traits like mindset, adaptability, and strategic thinking. For SDRs, the focus is on grit, creativity, and foundational sales skills, while for AEs, the emphasis is on advanced sales acumen and competitive positioning. Together, these structured interviews ensure you hire sales professionals who can excel in your unique environment and drive sustainable growth.

**Culture Fit Interview**

The final step is the culture fit interview, which takes place in a more casual setting. We invite candidates to an after-hours session where they teach us a game. It can be any game, even if we've all played it before. The point of the interview is to change their posture from interviewee to teacher. This relaxed environment allows us to observe how they interact with the team and whether they genuinely align with our values and culture. It's easy to fake answers to some of the interview questions, but it's much harder to pretend when you're forced into doing something silly like teaching people a game. The question we're asking ourselves at this stage is, "Will this person contribute to our culture and thrive within it?"

## How to Source Candidates

The best source for talent is referrals from people who already work for your company. When you have a high bar for talent, your team will understand that and help find candidates who can perform at that level.

When you're just starting out, you don't have that luxury. The next best source is referrals from people you've worked with before, customers, and investors.

When those wells run dry, your options are to post the job and run the process yourself, or hire a professional recruiter. There's no right answer here. Outsourcing will alleviate the burden of running the process, plus recruiters will generally have a pool of candidates they are working with, which might speed up the hire. But doing it internally will improve your team's ability and produce a better result at the end of the day.

## Spotting Raw Talent in the Unlikeliest Places

When Sarah first walked into our office, I remember mentally double-checking her résumé. Her most recent work experience? Two years of bar and café shifts peppered between auditions for film and theater roles. She had high grades from university, but in a field completely unrelated to sales. In other words, on paper, Sarah was not your classic SDR candidate.

Still, it took me all of fifteen minutes to realize this was someone special. She had a natural warmth that put our interview panel at ease almost immediately. We were talking about sales metrics one minute, and the next I was asking her to perform a recent monologue. Sarah didn't bat an eyelid. She stood up, took a breath, and delivered a short, intense scene from a play she had recently auditioned for. It might've been the most unconventional interview test I've ever given, but watching how fluently she shifted tone, managed the room, and maintained her composure told me everything I needed to know: This was an individual who could communicate under pressure, adapt on the fly, and connect with people in a genuine way.

In my experience, some of the best salespeople in the world come from unexpected backgrounds—bartenders, waiters, performers. They have abundant experience in serving and interacting with people, reading body language, and staying resilient even in the face of a hundred rejections. Sarah checked those boxes without having spent a single day in a formal sales role.

Over the next few months, she validated our instincts. Her first assignment—book a lot of meetings—wasn't just about volume; she brought an uncanny ability to read between the lines and tailor her message to each prospect. Before long, she was guest-hosting our company podcast, mentoring new SDRs, and consulting with our clients. In no time she became our top SDR, then our most effective SDR manager, and then joined our consulting team—helping clients implement the best practices she helped develop.

Sarah's path showed us that skills like tone, pacing, improvisation, and resilience often matter more than a classic sales résumé. That realization led her to develop a simple system to rate our SDRs on communication, diligence, and adaptability—uncovering a clear correlation to performance. Every quality that made Sarah stand out in her interview was right there on the list.

The takeaway? Look beyond bullet points and find what truly predicts success. If someone can confidently perform a monologue in front of strangers, they'll likely handle a tough sales call with poise. If they've juggled bartending shifts and theater auditions, they can certainly pivot in complex deals. Sarah's story remains one of my favorite reminders that raw talent, passion, and a willingness to learn can outshine even the most impressive track record in sales.

## The Onboarding Journey

Once you've made your hire, the real work begins. Bringing a salesperson up to speed isn't a quick handoff—it's a partnership. For the first few months, your new hire will lean heavily on you to learn the ropes. Expect to spend significant time coaching them and guiding them through the nuances of your product, market, and sales process.

This involves more than just handing over a playbook. Your new salesperson will need to understand your customer's pain points, how your product solves their problems, and how to effectively communicate your value proposition. Early on, this might include shadowing you on calls, meeting your customers, and revisiting the customer development process.

Even as they take on more responsibility, you'll still need to be actively involved. This means joining them on calls, providing feedback, and helping refine their approach. It's a time-intensive process, but one that pays dividends as your new hire gains confidence and starts to contribute independently.

For the first three months, expect to handle training your salesperson while still running the sales process yourself. You'll be sharing the workload—tag-teaming calls, reviewing their performance, and troubleshooting challenges. This can feel like a lot to manage, but it's critical for their development.

During this time, you'll

- teach them your sales process and ensure they're following it consistently;
- guide them in understanding your customers and their needs;
- review their calls, offering constructive feedback to help them improve; and
- meet regularly for one-on-ones to address questions, challenges, and goals.

The first 90 days are also when you'll build their confidence and set the tone for their future success. It's not uncommon for new salespeople to feel overwhelmed, especially if they're stepping into a founder-led sales process. Your support and clear guidance during this period will help them get through the learning curve and find their footing.

## How to Manage Salespeople

The role of a sales leader is to drive predictable results. This involves setting clear expectations, creating and reinforcing process, and maintaining a team of well-suited individuals. If you're a founder without a sales leader yet, guess what? That role is yours. Building a sales team requires process, consistency, and a commitment to learning. It may feel overwhelming, but mastering these fundamentals will help you build a team that not only meets targets, but thrives.

Being a great salesperson is about doing a bunch of little things right, over and over again. Process is the key to consistency. But a process is worthless without someone to teach, update, and reinforce it. This is the role a sales leader plays in manufacturing consistency.

A few years ago, we faced a serious sales problem. Our revenue team, usually consistent in hitting quota, ended both December and January at under 50 percent—a discouraging way to close and start a year. Before I dive into what happened, ask yourself: What would you do in this situation? Would you fire the rep immediately or give them a chance to turn it around?

This is a trick question. You don't yet have enough information to make an informed decision. As my mentor Joel Greensite would say, it's important to recognize whether you naturally default to being the "god of vengeance" or the "god of mercy." The truth is, good sales management lies in finding a balance between being firm on the fundamentals and soft on the human. Being firm means holding reps accountable when they miss targets and ensuring they understand the expectations. Being soft means providing them with the support and resources needed to overcome challenges.

When we first started Predictable Revenue, I struggled with this balance. I had a background in sales but little experience managing salespeople. If a rep wasn't performing, they either got too much leeway because I liked them or they were abruptly let go because I was frustrated. My leadership style often reflected my emotional state, which wasn't ideal for managing a team. For many founders this might sound familiar, especially if you're still learning sales yourself.

Over time, I learned the importance of diagnosing the root cause of performance issues. A key moment came when we hired Julian Marcuzzi, one of the best people managers I've ever worked with. Julian excelled at balancing firmness with empathy, and observing him helped me understand how to approach underperformance methodically. While Julian reported to me, I suspect I learned more from him than he did from me. He was our sales leader through some of the most difficult moments in Predictable Revenue's history and brought calm to the many storms we weathered together.

### Diagnosing a Problem

When dealing with a struggling rep, the first step is diagnosing whether the issue is a real problem or just a mathematical anomaly. For example, a rep might have pulled deals forward in one month, leading to a pipeline drought the next. By analyzing rolling averages for new leads, opportunities, and closed deals over 30, 90, and 180 days, you can spot trends and contextualize performance.

Next, evaluate lead and opportunity volume. If marketing had a bad month, your pipeline may have dried up, impacting results. Check conversion rates from leads to opportunities—changes here might indicate issues with lead quality or the qualification process. If external factors like seasonality or market conditions don't explain the dip, it's time to look internally.

When looking internally, I assess the problem across three dimensions: process, skills, and execution. Is the rep following the established process? Do they lack key skills or techniques? Are they putting in the necessary effort or are they burned out? I do this through a combination of call review, reviewing their metrics, and conversations with the rep. I often ask reps to share their worst calls for our team to review together because more senior reps will have a better idea of where they're getting stuck, while junior reps might not have a clue. Getting them to identify the problem gives me the opportunity to see how much they know about themselves and their own process. If need be, I'll spot-check additional calls to confirm whether the rep is accurately diagnosing their own issues.

### Coaching and Course Correction
If the problem is rooted in execution or confidence, the solution typically involves a mix of role-playing, training, and self-study. For example, in a role-playing session I might have the rep act as themselves while I play the prospect. Afterward we reverse roles, helping them see the conversation from both sides. Training sessions focus on key learning objectives and provide structured feedback, while self-study reinforces new concepts through homework like documenting their process for future reps.

It's also important to set clear expectations. Document the issue, the steps needed to resolve it, and the potential consequences of failing to improve. I follow a "no surprises" termination process, starting with a verbal warning, escalating to a written warning, and only then considering dismissal. This typically spans three months, though timelines may vary depending on the sales cycle.

### Avoiding Common Pitfalls
It's easy to let reps blame the market when results dip. However, unless you have conclusive evidence of external factors, this approach only delays solving the real problem. Often, confidence issues are symptoms of gaps in process or skills. Digging deeper is critical. Performance management is about more than diagnosing and addressing issues—it's about maintaining a culture of accountability and support. Firing underperformers without fully understanding the root cause erodes team morale and culture. Conversely, giving too much leeway to struggling reps without addressing underlying issues risks dragging the

team down. Sometimes, the problem isn't with the sales team but the product, competition, or market conditions. Founders must take responsibility for these variables instead of blaming sales leadership. If your company isn't hitting revenue targets, start by examining these broader factors before making personnel changes.

### The Three Meetings

Sales leadership revolves around creating consistency, and these three core meetings—Pipeline Review, Call Review, and One-on-Ones—are how you do it. Think of them like unit tests written for software: They confirm that the things that are supposed to be happening are indeed happening as expected. These meetings are the glue that holds your sales process together, ensuring your team consistently delivers results. We do these regularly to maintain consistency and hopefully catch issues early before they become larger problems.

**1. Pipeline Review: The foundation of forecast accuracy.** The pipeline review is all about ensuring your forecast is reliable and grounded in reality. This meeting focuses on deals likely to close in the next 30 days. By sorting your opportunity list in descending order (latest stage at the top), you work systematically through your pipeline, focusing on the deals closest to closing.

Ask key questions for each late-stage deal:

- Is there a next step with the prospect on the calendar?
- Does the qualification score meet or exceed 90%?
- Have stage entry and exit criteria been met?

If "do nothing" is off the table for the prospect, pay special attention to why: Urgency is a key driver of successful closes. For deals that pass these hygiene checks, ask your rep whether they believe the deal will close this month or next. This judgment call feeds into your forecast probabilities:

- 80%: verbal agreement and scheduled to close this month
- 50%: passed hygiene and expected to close next month

This meeting isn't just about identifying deals that are ready to close; it's also an opportunity to spot gaps in the pipeline and adjust strategy. If the pipeline-to-quota ratio isn't where it needs to be (ideally 1.2x quota for late-stage deals), you know where to focus your team's efforts.

By sticking to this method, you create a consistent framework for forecasting that reduces decision fatigue and minimizes errors. It's less about guesswork and more about following a clear, repeatable process.

**2. Call Review: A weekly opportunity for feedback and growth.** Every week I ask my reps to bring me call recordings to listen to, their best and their worst. My goal is to find one area for improvement for next week and one win from this week to celebrate. I like to start with the worst call first so we can end on a positive note.

When I first started doing these, I acted like it was a driving test, taking note of every tiny mistake no matter how insignificant. When we finished listening to the call, I would have a list of the 37 things they screwed up. To make matters worse, I once let a class of MBAs sit in on a call-review session (sorry Jason). Needless to say, this approach wasn't helpful and over time I took a successful rep and murdered their confidence, leaving them looking for another job.

Fortunately, I suck at golf, which led me to watch a video where an instructor and student were at the driving range. At first, the instructor watched a few drives and listed the seven things the student needed to change for their next swing. It didn't go well. Next, they tried again but this time only shared one thing to change. These drives went significantly better. The video was obviously staged but it resonated so strongly with me that it's burned into my memory. Our goal as leaders is to identify all the areas a rep needs to improve, prioritize them, and only share the one with the highest potential impact for them to work on that week.

Use call reviews to identify patterns, address skill gaps, and reinforce the behaviors that lead to success. Done right, these sessions become a source of motivation and clarity for your reps.

**3. One-on-Ones: Managing the human side of sales.** While pipeline and call reviews focus on deals and skills, one-on-ones are about the human side of sales. Salespeople are people first, and their emotions, energy, and mindset directly impact performance. This meeting is your chance to check in on both their personal and professional well-being.

Each one-on-one should have three goals:

- **Connect:** Ensure the rep is doing well both personally and professionally.
- **Remind:** Revisit their goals and development plans to keep them focused on the bigger picture.
- **Unblock:** Identify and resolve any obstacles, whether it's a stuck deal, a process issue, or a team dynamic.

These meetings are also an opportunity to celebrate small wins and keep your team motivated. By balancing accountability with encouragement, you can help your reps stay focused and engaged.

Together, these three meetings create a rhythm of consistency that drives predictable results. They ensure your process is being followed, your team is continuously improving, and your reps have the support they need to thrive. Think of them as your quality control system—your way of making sure the sales engine you're building runs smoothly and efficiently.

With a solid structure in place, you'll not only set your team up for success but also free yourself from the constant firefighting that comes with a poorly managed sales process. These meetings are your investment in building a high-performing, scalable sales team.

You've now seen how to move from "selling everything yourself" to leading a new salesperson—and eventually an entire team—without losing what made your product special in the first place. Embrace these processes for documenting your success, hiring effectively, and managing with clear structure. Yes, it can feel daunting, but keep leaning on these strategies and you'll find it's the best way for even the most sleep-deprived founder to guide their company to real, predictable revenue.

# TYING IT ALL TOGETHER

**C**ONGRATULATIONS! You've made it all the way. And you may have noticed that the terrifying art of finding customers and building revenue isn't a simple matter of sales. It's ultimately about prioritization and strategy—and process, good process, lots of good process.

What's next? A whole lot, believe me. The work of building revenue is never truly done, but you've now got the tools to tackle it with confidence and clarity. As you move forward, remember this: Finding customers is not just about the next deal or campaign—it's about creating value, solving real problems, and forging connections that last.

This is the end of this book, but it's just the beginning of your journey. You'll refine your strategies, adjust your processes, and learn as you go. Along the way, you'll face new challenges, but you'll also uncover new opportunities. To keep growing, keep learning.

You've got this. Go out there, take some risks, and keep learning from your customers. The terrifying art gets a little less terrifying with every step you take.

Here's to your success.

Before you go, here's a reminder of what we covered:

## Action Steps

**1. Find pain that's shared by many.** The more painful and widespread the problem you solve, the easier your GTM strategy becomes. Focus your efforts on high-importance, low-satisfaction problems.

**2. Use a customer development funnel.** Start small. This stage is all about learning and earning. Create your first customers by understanding their pain, learning from people, and proving your value.

**3. Don't scale prematurely.** Avoid the trap of investing in growth too soon. Ensure you've validated your product and your process before scaling—it's critical to have something worth investing in.

**4. Embrace the sales role.** Nobody knows your customers' pain or your product better than you. Use what you've learned in the customer development process to become your company's best salesperson.

**5. Focus on building strong sales habits.** Developing habits, reflecting on your efforts, and refining your process are more important than any single sale. A solid process is the foundation for long-term success.

**6. Invest in growth at the right time.** Make sure every growth investment is well timed and backed by a thoughtful model. Understanding funnel math and alignment is key to scaling efficiently.

**7. Treat growth as a chain-link system.** Your business's growth is only as strong as its weakest link. You can't outrun churn or achieve your full potential without every part of your system firing on all cylinders.

**8. Document and do it yourself.** By building and documenting the processes yourself, you'll ensure your team's success when you hand the processes off.

**9. Hire for leverage.** Hire people who enable you to work *on* the business instead of getting stuck *in* it. Build a team that complements your strengths and grows with your vision.

## The Journey Ahead

This book has equipped you with the principles, strategies, and processes to build a revenue engine that scales. But the work is never done. Markets shift, customer needs evolve, and challenges will continue to arise. Stay curious, keep learning, and never stop refining your craft.

As you move forward, remember: The terrifying art of finding customers isn't about quick wins—it's about mastering the balance of strategy, timing, and execution. You've already proven you can handle the terrifying part. Now it's time to go make it extraordinary.

Because building a thriving business means embracing new challenges and opportunities at every stage, you'll find yourself returning to these principles—prioritization, strategy, and process—time and again as you scale. As your business evolves, so will your role. You'll shift from being the sole driver to being the architect of a system that can thrive without you.

To help you along the way, here are a few books that have shaped my thinking and might guide you in the next leg of your journey:

***Who: The A Method for Hiring* by Geoff Smart and Randy Street**
This book helped me realize I was hiring like an idiot. My customer lifetime doubled after I used what I learned in this book

to improve my hiring process. Anyone who's worked for Carb.io or Predictable Revenue has this book to thank for the wonderful people who work there.

### *Good Strategy/Bad Strategy* by Richard P. Rumelt

I used to think that quarterly planning, where we set big hairy goals and built action plans to achieve them, was strategy work. It's not. This book helped me realize what real strategy work looks like. Rumelt has another book called *The Crux* that is also exceptional, but I'll always have a soft spot for this one. My copy is beat to hell with notes, Post-its, and bent pages from being carried everywhere I went for an entire year.

### *7 Powers* by Hamilton Helmer

*Good Strategy/Bad Strategy* helped me realize I wasn't doing strategic work and *7 Powers* helped me understand what my strategic work should be focusing on: producing persistent differential returns.

### *The Messy Middle* by Scott Belsky

Scott's book resonated more than any entrepreneur's book ever has. Not only was it raw and honest, it provided actionable guidance.

### *Obviously Awesome* by April Dunford

Reading this changed the way I thought about crafting messaging. It's an exceptional book on the strategic work of positioning and also an extremely helpful tactical guide to creating great sales and marketing campaigns.

### *The Mom Test* by Rob Fitzpatrick and *The Lean Product Playbook* by Dan Olsen

These books got me unstuck after voltageCRM failed. I couldn't figure out why nobody wanted to buy my crappy CRM system, and these books helped me understand that I wasn't really listening to people.

***The New Strategic Selling* by Robert B. Miller and Stephen E. Heiman**
There aren't many sales books out there that aren't regurgitating at least a little Miller Heiman. This one's a slow read but contains almost everything you need to know about enterprise selling. Reading this book was like that moment in *The Wizard of Oz* where everything went from black and white to color.

***Lean Customer Development* by Cindy Alvarez**
I've watched Cindy's interview on Mixergy at least 100 times. Her work was my first exposure to the craft of customer development and her book helped me develop the skills needed to find the Carb.io opportunity. Cindy was also kind enough to sit down with me for this book and share some additional pieces that refined the customer development sections.

***Predictable Revenue* by Aaron Ross**
I wouldn't be an entrepreneur without Aaron or his book. He was kind and generous when I cold-emailed (stalked) him with questions and was a solid business partner when we worked together. This book put sales teams in the spotlight again and inspired a gold rush of investment in sales technology.

EACH OF these books complements the principles we've covered here and offers insights to deepen your knowledge of strategy, growth, and leadership.

You've taken on the terrifying art of finding customers, and you've come out stronger, smarter, and better equipped to lead your company to new heights. Keep experimenting, keep learning, and most importantly, keep building.

Thank you for letting me be part of your journey. Now go out there and make it happen!

# FOUNDER SUMMARY

## Chapter 1: The Only Thing That Matters

This chapter sets the foundation for the entire startup journey by laying out three critical steps:

1. Find a gap in the market that matches your strengths and solves a high-importance, low-satisfaction problem.

2. Identify and engage with the people who will actually pay you for your solution.

3. Build a system that makes revenue repeatable.

By focusing on these steps in the right order, you ensure real product-market fit before scaling, set yourself up to move from learning into selling gracefully, and finally create a revenue engine that can grow even when you're not directly involved.

## Chapter 2: Finding Product-Market Fit

In this chapter, we see that product-market fit (PMF) is neither permanent nor a simple yes/no—it's all about the strength of the way you solve a critical, unmet need. When you truly have PMF, it feels like momentum carries you forward effortlessly; customers seek you out, excitement builds through referrals, and usage grows despite an incomplete product. If there are similar products in the market, finding your 10x edge is vital—your solution has to be 10 times better, because a small margin isn't enough to compel buyers to switch. Ultimately, PMF requires honest discovery, testing of real customer pain, and ongoing validation as the market and product evolve.

**Action Steps**

1 **Search for a 10x difference:** Identify whether your idea solves a previously untouched problem or addresses an existing one in a way that's at least 10 times better than your competitors'.

2 **Quantify unmet needs:** Use exploratory interviews to ask open-ended questions, then drill down with importance and satisfaction ratings to find high-pain, low-satisfaction gaps.

3 **Watch for momentum signals:** Look for genuine excitement, organic referrals, and early willingness to use your product—even when it's incomplete—as proof you're on the right track.

## Chapter 3: Your First Customers

This chapter dives into how your early customer development interviews naturally become your first source of paying customers—if you've uncovered a true "hair-on-fire" problem, people will be keen to buy. It's a delicate balance between learning and selling because you're refining your product while testing revenue possibilities in real time. By moving people systematically through Exploratory, Focused, Paper Feedback, and MVP Demo interviews, you slowly shift the context from learning to selling. If nobody from your interviews is ready to pay or refer others, it's time to revisit your assumptions—because strong product-market fit means customers will pull the solution out of you.

### Action Steps

1 **Work your customer development funnel:** Build momentum by inviting people to the next stage in your funnel—if they're truly "on fire," they'll jump at the chance to proceed.

2 **Stay in listening mode:** Make sure at least 90 percent of your calls focus on understanding pain points; only then should you discuss your product.

3 **Look for genuine pull:** Watch for early signals like referrals to other people you can interview, customers physically leaning in, and that "ahhh" sound people make when they finally get it. If no one's eager, keep refining before investing in building the product or trying to grow.

## Chapter 4: Getting Ready for Growth

In this chapter, we see the high-stakes transition from finding product-market fit to scaling successfully—and how rushing growth can backfire. With Carb.io, my initial spike in demand turned sour when technical issues and competitor pressure eroded referrals. The Growth Formula (cash invested × PMF strength × revenue execution × power) underscores the delicate balance between your product's pull, the resources you have, and the efficiency of your sales engine. You can't just buy growth or rely on a brief wave of interest; you need to solidify your product, keep listening to customers, and methodically test each market segment. Document your chain of relevance (market, needs, solution) and make sure your early adopters are truly satisfied—otherwise, you risk burning through momentum and missing your real window to scale.

**Action Steps**

1. **Keep PMF strong:** Don't let feature bloat or technical debt overshadow customer needs. Prioritize usability and reliability to maintain (and deepen) product-market fit.

2. **Use the Growth Formula wisely:** Track where weak links might be holding you back (cash, PMF strength, or revenue execution), and address those gaps before doubling down on growth spend.

3. **Document and communicate learnings:** Define your target segments, their unmet needs, and how you solve them. This shared chain of relevance ensures your team and future hires stay aligned.

4. **Confirm willingness to pay:** Even in early versions, ask for at least *some* money. If prospects resist, treat it as a signal to revisit your assumptions rather than plowing ahead with scaling plans.

## Chapter 5: How to Sell

This chapter debunks the myth that "real sales professionals" are the only ones who can close deals and shows how founders—already experts in the problem space—are often the best early sales reps. You don't need manipulative tactics; you need empathy, a strong process, and genuine concern for whether your product solves the customer's biggest pain. By treating the sales conversation as a logical exploration of their situation—diagnosing their problem, recommending a solution, and suggesting next steps—you help prospects make the best decision, even if it isn't you. Done right, sales is simply a continuation of customer development, guided by the principle that your true job is to help people, not just chase outcomes.

### Action Steps

1 **Focus on real problems:** Confirm that each prospect truly has the unmet needs you solve. If their pain isn't clear—or you can't address it—avoid forcing a deal that won't last.

2 **Structure the conversation:** Use the four-step "situation, diagnosis, recommendation, action" framework to ensure you fully understand their context before offering a solution.

3 **Detach from the outcome:** Embrace Stoic principles—control the process, not the prospect's final decision. Concentrate on honest discovery and alignment instead of pressuring for a yes.

4 **Guide, don't pitch:** Present alternative paths and educate prospects on the pros and cons of each. Show why yours might be the best fit, but don't hide it if it isn't.

5 **Keep next steps clear:** Always schedule a follow-up or outline agreed-upon actions. Reliability and consistency (the "do:say ratio") build trust and prevent deals from stalling.

## Chapter 6: Sales Habits

This chapter emphasizes that great sales results come from consistent habits, not secret tricks or naturally gifted closers. You'll sell more effectively by tailoring each conversation to the unique problem a prospect needs solved, rather than pushing a generic pitch. Simple routines like booking your next call before ending the current one, documenting a "next action" and "next action date" for every opportunity, and regularly reviewing your recorded calls for feedback can dramatically increase your close rates. Ultimately, these habits form the bedrock of a scalable sales process you'll refine and pass on as you grow your team.

### Action Steps

1. **Ditch the pre-built pitch:** Avoid leading with slides or screenshares. Instead, open by asking questions that uncover the real change your prospect needs.

2. **Lock in next steps live:** Always schedule your follow-up call before ending the current one—this one habit saves time, keeps deals moving, and reveals who's truly serious.

3. **Use "next action" fields:** Record what you'll do next and by when in your CRM or spreadsheet so that you can revisit each deal quickly without losing momentum.

4. **Review call recordings:** Analyze your tone, questions asked, and how prospects responded. Share recordings with mentors or cofounders for fresh insights and faster improvement.

## Chapter 7: How to Build Your First Channel

In this chapter, we take a hard look at how to build your first scalable, repeatable channel. There are only four ways to grow—referrals, upsell/expansion, earned, and paid—and each has different costs, timelines, and risks. Whether you're considering influencer marketing, tapping a partner network, or spinning up outbound sales, success boils down to methodically testing for "proof of life," then optimizing, and only doubling down once it's profitable. Crucially, do the math before you invest (for example, calculate how many deals you'll need to cover costs), and think twice about quick-fix outsourcing, which rarely works unless you give it enough time, training, and a well-defined market.

**Action Steps**

1 **Map your growth paths:** Decide how you'll balance referrals, upsell, earned tactics (outbound, SEO), and paid channels—don't spread yourself too thin.

2 **Stage your channel tests:** Start small to prove there's real potential, optimize your approach, then scale only when you can turn a profit.

3 **Run the numbers:** Calculate customer acquisition cost, required deal flow, and payback time up front—without solid math, you'll waste resources on channels that can't deliver return on investment.

4 **Own your GTM team:** Resist "outsource-and-hope" fixes. Building in-house means better alignment, deeper product knowledge, and more consistent results over the long term.

## Chapter 8: Four Funnels That Drive Growth

In this chapter, we discover that creating sustainable growth depends on four specialized funnels—Meet, Disco, Manage, and Nurture—all working together like links in a chain. When even one funnel is weak (like ignoring long-term prospects or failing to retain current customers), your entire growth engine stalls. By splitting pipelines into clear, outcome-based stages and applying a shared qualification method (MEDDPICC, for example), you keep each funnel organized and accurate. This clarity not only prevents deals from slipping through the cracks but also enables stronger forecasting and a more focused, nimble approach—often without needing a complex CRM system.

**Action Steps**

1 **Specialize your funnels:** Allocate different pipelines or at least distinct views for each function (Meet, Disco, Manage, Nurture), ensuring no single pipeline is overloaded with dead or future opportunities.

2 **Establish objective stages:** Use externally verifiable outcomes (such as "Meeting Booked" or "Customer Attended Discovery Call") to define your stages so that there's no guesswork in your sales process.

3 **Score deals consistently:** Adopt a qualification framework and use simple scoring (0–2) for each criterion to track what you actually know about a deal and identify the best next action.

## Chapter 9: Hire and Manage Your First Salesperson

In this chapter you learn how to step away from founder-led sales and scale revenue through your first hire—without losing the passion, insight, and credibility you bring to every deal. Handing over the reins involves documenting exactly what makes your sales approach work, then using a structured hiring method (like the WHO process) to find the right fit. Once your new rep is on board, you'll sustain their success by running regular pipeline reviews, call reviews, and one-on-ones, ensuring they steadily absorb your expertise and deliver the consistent results you need to reach that million-dollar milestone and beyond.

## Action Steps

1 **Document your playbook:** Outline each sales stage, buyer persona, and key objection-handling strategy so that your new rep can replicate (and scale) your success.

2 **Adopt a structured hiring process:** Use a proven method to evaluate candidates thoroughly—no shortcuts—and focus on traits like curiosity, grit, and culture fit.

3 **Manage with consistency:** Hold weekly pipeline and call reviews, plus one-on-one check-ins, to reinforce best practices, track progress, and support your new hire's growth.

# ACKNOWLEDGMENTS

A SPECIAL THANKS to everyone below, without whose help this book would not have been possible:

My family, Nikki, Neil, and Joe for your support and encouragement while I was writing this book. To my parents for, well... making me. To my brother for being my bro, a fellow entrepreneur, and a good friend. If you're interested in handcrafted soaps made with all-natural ingredients, check him out: sodacreeksoap.com.

My voltageCRM, Carb.io, and Predictable Revenue cofounders Preston, Francesco, and Aaron. I learned an immense amount from all of you because I got to make all the mistakes.

My editor, the (*editor's note: exceptionally talented yet still modest*) individual who had to read all of these words before they were any good. James, this book would be a pile of trash without your help (*editor's note: no, it would still have been a gold mine, but not everyone would have dug it*).

Trena, the first person who believed I actually might pull off writing a decent book. Thanks for all your help before I was a client and ever since.

All the people who had to suffer under my leadership while I learned how to be a founder and then a CEO. Thank you for your patience, tolerance, and guidance.

The Predictable Revenue team past, present, and future. And our customers, especially in cases where everything seemed to go wrong—I learned the most from you.

Dan, Bob, John, and the whole Ames family—I'm eternally grateful you gave me that first chance.

Everyone involved in the team effort behind building Market-Fit: Aaron's Niche Matrix, which was refined by many account strategists at Predictable Revenue (including Jerry, Patrick, Cole, Niamh, Ashley, Jonathan, Ania, and Nicola), and ultimately perfected by Kenny MacKenzie. Thank you all.

Thank you to Michel Feaster for our many conversations on creating categories, customer development, and the startup journey. These conversations opened my eyes and helped shape this book.

Thank you to Cindy Alvarez for that video on Mixergy that I must have watched a hundred times and for taking the time to sit down with me and walk me through the finer points of customer development.

Thank you to Lars Nilsson for our conversations on the history of sales development, your journey at Cloudera, and the early sales journey.

Thank you to every *Predictable Revenue Podcast* guest. This book wouldn't exist without the over 400 interviews that served as my sales PhD.

Everyone at the Page Two team, thank you for helping make this book worth reading.

All the entrepreneurs who have taken time out of their day to help me figure things out. I'd still have one customer for voltageCRM if it weren't for you all.

To my founder friends who shared their feedback, argued with me, read/re-read, and everything else related to this book.

James Clift, Matt Smith, Michael Tuso, Kenny MacKenzie, Karl Holmqvist, Kareem Mayan, Jay Mount, Megan Wilson, Sarah Hicks, Julian Marcuzzi, Darius Lahoutifard, Mark Hunter, Fred Diamond, and everyone else who helped.

And lastly a huge thank-you to everyone on the Founder's Edition newsletter (foundersedition.co) and especially anyone who's ever replied to one of my posts. I always value our back-and-forths, and your comments made this book better (apologies if I missed you):

Aaron B, Aaron G, Aaron R, Adam B, Adam H, Adam L, Adam M, Adam S, Adishesh K, Adrian M, Akhil S, Alan M, Albert D, Alberto G, Alberto P, Alex L, Alex V, Alfredo G, Ali K, Ali T, Alistair M, Aliya B, Allen N, Aloke N, Amanda B, Amanda M, Amanda S, Ammanuel S, Anatoly S, Andre S, Andre V, Andrew B, Andrew C, Andrew D, Andrew S, Andrew T, Andy M, Andy W, Angelo F, Anish M, Anne C, Anthony B, Anthony S, Aparna R, Arslan N, Ashley C, Ashley K, Ashley M, Ashley M, Astrid S, Axhens M, Aye M, Beau A, Ben B, Ben S, Benjamin B, Benjamin L, Bentz E, Besart C, Bhavya A, Bill H, Bill R, Billi R, Bob D, Bobby N, Boris B, Brad G, Brandi H, Brandon G, Brandon S, Brant C, Brenda N, Brenda W, Brendan J, Brent J, Brent S, Brett T, Brian A, Brian C, Brian D, Brian F, Brian G, Brian J, Brian S, Brooke V, Caleb S, Carly S, Carmen H, Casey P, Cash B, Celeste D, Chad M, Chase C, Chase S, Chastin R, Cherechi O, Chicke F, Chitra G, Chris A, Chris E, Chris G, Chris H, Chris K, Chris M, Chris M, Chris M, Chris O, Chris S, Christian A, Christian G, Christine L, Christopher C, Christopher M, Chuck D, Chuck M, Clayton T, Colin R, Collin T, Cooper M, Craig R, Cyrus M, Daiyaan I, Dan E, Dan M, Dan W, Dana B, Dana K, Daniel F, Daniel I, Daniel S, Daniele D, Darius L, Dave E, Dave W, David B, David C, David F, David J, David K, David M, David P, David W, Denis L, Denise M, Dennis H, Denny D, Derek L, Devin M, Dexter K, Dexter W, Dori W, Dottie J, Douglas D, Dr M, Edward I, Eli P, Elon B, Emad I, Emil J, Eric F, Eric G, Eric N, Eric W, Erik G, Erik J, Erika B,

Ethan E, Ethan S, Ewing G, Fengmin G, Feynman L, Francie J, Frank Z, Fred L, Fred S, Frederick A, Fryderyk W, Gavin P, Georgii K, Gianluca P, Gina B, Glenn M, Graeham F, Gregg H, Guru T, Hamid A, Harmat G, Harvey S, Hassan E, Hays W, Heather A, Heather H, Helen Z, Holli H, Hrishi V, Hugo E, Iain F, Ibrahim A, Ilya B, Isaac R, Isaiah U, Jack B, Jacob B, Jacob H, Jacob M, Jake K, Jake W, James D, James E, James H, Jamie C, Jamie R, Jamie T, Janine O, Jared T, Jarred D, Jason B, Jason D, Jason G, Jason M, Jason S, Jason W, Javier D, Jay K, Jay M, Jay M, Jean-Francois B, Jeff D, Jeff K, Jeff S, Jeremy M, Jeron A, Jerrard S, Jess B, Jesse H, Jessica B, Jessica K, Jim H, Jim L, Jim M, Joe A, Joel Z, John C, John D, John K, John M, John M, Jon C, Jon F, Jon W, Jonas S, Jonathan G, Jonathan J, Jordan P, Jose M, Joseph M, Josh B, Josh T, Judah P, Julia C, Julian L, Julian W, Julie R, Justin C, Justin S, Karen S, Katelyn E, Kathy S, Kaustubh M, Keel R, Keisha H, Keith G, Keith N, Kelson Q, Ken P, Kent M, Kent S, Kevin D, Kevin M, Kim C, Kincy C, Kirsti T, Kodie C, Kody K, Kreg M, Kristen C, Kristopher K, Ksenia S, Lamine B, Laura B, Laura C, Leavett B, Leopoldo P, Les O, Lirel H, Lisa H, Liz S, Lori C, Louis K, Mac S, Madhu A, Manoj D, Marc T, Margo P, Marie D, Mark C, Mark D, Mark G, Mark H, Mark L, Mark P, Mark W, Marty A, Mase I, Matt H, Matt M, Matt W, Matthew B, Matthew D, Matthew G, Mauricio A, Max E, Max M, Maxim M, Meghan C, Meredith B, Michael B, Michael F, Michael G, Michael L, Michael P, Mike B, Mike R, Milan T, Miroslav P, Mordy K, Morgan L, Mustafa B, Nara S, Nathan S, Nathan T, Neda V, Neil K, Nic S, Nick E, Nick S, Nico F, Nicole G, Nigel E, Noah M, Norman O, Om P, Patrick D, Patrick H, Paul G, Paul K, Paul P, Paul S, Paul Z, Perry M, Peter O, Petr K, Phil D, Pierre T, Pormer S, Prabhakar R, Prakash M, Prakash S, Prasad A, Radim R, Rado K, Raghav G, Rajesh K, Ramon S, Rand A, Randy D, Randy F, Ray M, Raza R, Remi B, Rich H, Richard D, Richard G, Richard N, Richard Y, Rick B, Rick V, Riku I, Rob A, Robert A, Robert C, Robert J, Robert L, Roberto

A, Robin M, Rockwell F, Rodrigo L, Roman S, Rose H, Ruddens B, Ryan H, Ryan T, Sam E, Sam K, Sam M, Sam Z, Sammy J, Sandy R, Sara H, Scott H, Scott R, Scott Y, Sean M, Sean S, Sergio M, Shane R, Shaun K, Sherry C, Shervin J, Shishir R, Shlomi S, Shmuel S, Siloh M, Simon W, Skyler R, Sofi S, Sonja B, Sophia O, Stan P, Stefan B, Stephanie C, Stephanie M, Stephanie S, Steve D, Steve F, Steve M, Steven P, Steven T, Steven W, Stuart D, Stuart W, Sundar B, Sunil M, Suresh K, Susan A, Sushant S, Suzan B, Tareq A, Ted W, Tejasvin S, Thiv P, Thomas S, Tierra L, Tighe B, Tim H, Tina B, Tod N, Todd K, Tom B, Tom H, Tomaz S, Tracy G, Tregg F, Trena W, Trevor H, Trip F, Troy M, Tzachi B, Ulrik S, Varsha W, Varun S, Ved P, Venkat R, Victoria P, Vig A, Viola R, Vishnu T, Vitalii M, Vladimir L, Vladyslav D, Vytenis P, Walter H, Walton L, Warren N, Wayne K, Wendi D, Wenqin C, Wes K, Will G, Willem M, William B, William N, Yannick C, Yichen J, Yooni A, Zeal C, Zheng L, Zhenni J, Ziad K.

# ADDITIONAL RESOURCES

YOU CAN find a list of the free resources I've mentioned throughout the book at terrifyingart.com/resources:

- our internal sales hiring guide
- a sales math sheet
- a customer development cheat sheet
- a PDF of the four funnels
- our MarketFit Matrix (and some training resources)
- a PDF of the founder summary from the previous chapter

Here are some resources that I'll trade you for your email:

- a custom GPT with the full text of this book in it
- a GPT to pull jobs-to-be-done statements from interview transcripts
- a Clay.com template that verifies a list of target companies and prospects meet your ICP
- a free PDF of Aaron Ross's book *Predictable Revenue*

Here are some pieces that might be helpful that we charge for:

- the Terrifying Art of Finding Customers course
- the Founder revenue coaching service
- building cool stuff with Clay.com
- coaching and consulting related to building outbound sales teams

Check them out at terrifyingart.com/more.

THANKS FOR reading, and feel free to email me at collin@terrifyingart.com with any questions or comments.

# Predictable Revenue

Predictable Revenue is a revenue consulting company dedicated to helping founders achieve sustainable, efficient, and predictable growth.

We believe that strong product-market fit is the foundation of lasting success and that great companies thrive by deeply understanding and solving real customer needs.

We create tailored strategies and practical frameworks that empower founders to uncover market opportunities, build effective sales teams, and accelerate their path to scalable revenue.

Learn more at **predictablerevenue.com**.

Stay updated with Collin's latest projects and insights at **foundersedition.co.**

# ABOUT COLLIN STEWART

I'M COLLIN, and my passion is helping founders land their first customers. My journey in sales began at just five years old, right after my family moved to a new city. My parents sent me door-to-door to find kids my age to play with, and two cul-de-sacs later, I met my buddy Jordan. We've been friends ever since.

When I started voltageCRM, I knew how to sell—but I had no idea what to build or how to build it. Interestingly, most founders have the opposite problem: They're excellent builders but struggle with sales. What many don't realize is that selling isn't about imposing something on someone; it naturally occurs when you identify and fill a genuine gap in their professional lives.

I love helping founders discover those gaps and build teams capable of connecting with everyone who experiences them.

I've been fortunate to witness strong product-market fit both firsthand and through my clients. I was Uber's first call when they set up their initial B2B sales team, and I've also been the first call for several Uber imitators that didn't succeed. I helped Toptal establish their first sales development team and watched them exceed every benchmark. Conversely, I've also seen hundreds of competitive marketplaces and outsourced development shops struggle to get positive responses. These contrasting

experiences have taught me the significance of finding a truly worthwhile market gap.

In 2014, my software company Carb.io merged with Aaron Ross's PebbleStorm, and I became the CEO of a book—and the company now known as Predictable Revenue. At Predictable Revenue, we help founders strengthen their product-market fit, driving resilient, efficient, and predictable revenue growth. You can learn more at predictablerevenue.com.

As a keynote speaker, I blend pragmatic advice, humor, and candid stories about both my successes and (many) failures. I've spoken at venues ranging from my bathroom mirror to global SaaS conferences like Dreamforce, SAAS NORTH, and Acetech Whistler. You can learn more at meetcollin.com.

To stay updated on my latest projects, writings, or tools, subscribe to my Founder's Edition newsletter at foundersedition.co, or check out my podcast at podcast.terrifyingart.com.

I also host a monthly founders call focused on collaboratively solving revenue challenges—from achieving product-market fit to accelerating growth. It's currently free for founders under $1 million in revenue, though that might change in the future. Interested? Apply here: terrifyingart.com/meetup.